A PHILOSOPHY OF LYING

A Philosophy of Lying

Lars Svendsen

Translated by
Matt Bagguley

REAKTION BOOKS

Published by Reaktion Books Ltd
Unit 32, Waterside
44–48 Wharf Road
London n1 7ux, uk
www.reaktionbooks.co.uk

First published in English 2022
English-language translation © Reaktion Books 2022

Matt Bagguley asserts his moral right to be
identified as the translator of the work

This book was first published in Norwegian in 2020 by Kagge Forlag AS
under the title *Løgnens filosofi* by Lars H. Fr. Svendsen
Copyright © Lars H. Fr. Svendsen 2020
Published in agreement with Oslo Literary Agency
All rights reserved

This translation has been published
with the financial support of NORLA

Printed and bound in Great Britain by Bell & Bain, Glasgow

A catalogue record for this book is available from the British Library

ISBN 978 1 78914 563 2

Contents

Introduction

Not that you lied to me,
but that I no longer believe you,
has shaken me.

FRIEDRICH NIETZSCHE, *Beyond Good and Evil*

Everyone lies. Everyone condemns lying. We lie even though we agree that lying is wrong. We lie for our own benefit, to appear better – or less bad – than we are, to get an advantage or to spare ourselves trouble and discomfort. We also lie for someone else's benefit, to spare their feelings or avoid hurting them. It's often hard to tell whether we are lying for someone else's sake or our own – we like to tell ourselves that it is for someone else's sake, but even that often involves us lying to ourselves.

I can't remember when I told my first lie, nor what I was lying about. It was probably when I was three or four years old, because that's when we humans start doing that sort of thing, and it was probably to avoid being blamed for doing something wrong. I have never been a very good liar. My father, however, was a formidable liar. They weren't malicious lies, just pranks, and my brother and I fell for them almost every damn time. My mother, on the other hand, saw through him most of the time. I almost never managed to fool anyone with a lie. One of the downsides of being the youngest in a family is that everyone else has a psychological advantage

7

over you. That could explain why I never became a skilled liar – I was so rarely successful that I lacked the inspiration to continue.

Nevertheless, I didn't quit completely. Since becoming aware of the possibility of lying, I have lied to everyone I've had a relationship with. I have lied to my parents, brother, wife, girlfriends, children, friends and colleagues. After this admission, however, I feel the sudden need to sugarcoat the pill by saying that on the whole I have been honest with them all. Honesty is not necessarily just an expression of a good character, but is also due to the fact that life is easier when you are honest. A liar has to remember twice as much as someone who is telling the truth – both how something really is and how he has said it is. I prefer an uncomplicated life. In this sense, honesty is as much to do with my own convenience as it is about morality. Considering merely one's own convenience, however, is a poor foundation on which to build one's moral life.

Of all the lies I have told, I like to think that most of them have been 'white', in that I have tried to protect someone directly by being untruthful towards them, or indirectly by telling beneficial lies to someone else about them. However, I've also told quite a few of the 'grey' or even 'black' variety, where the only consideration I had was for myself – where telling the truth would have created more discomfort or problems for me than telling a lie. Hopefully I have mostly avoided the really coal-black lies, where you knowingly and intentionally hurt someone else by telling a lie. My white lies have probably been in the majority. Does that mean that what I have done is okay? Is it morally acceptable to tell white lies? Of course, it is also conceivable that I suffer from such an acute level of self-deception that I am hiding the extent of my dishonesty from myself. But I don't believe that either.

Most people are truthful in general. The majority tell far fewer lies than the average person because there is a minority among us who raise this average steeply.[1] In the grand scheme of things, lies make up a very small part of everything we say to each other. However, this doesn't mean that lying is not a phenomenon of great importance. One lie, if serious enough, can ruin a marriage, a friendship, a career or a life.

Today's philosophical discussions about lying revolve chiefly around the question of what lies *are*, about what makes a lie a lie, and what distinguishes it from other related phenomena. These discussions are predominantly found in the philosophy of language.[2] I will address these questions, but there are more ethical issues at the heart of my research. There is comprehensive research on lying in social psychology, but I will only be considering this to a small extent.[3] Nevertheless, some findings in this research can be mentioned briefly here. People lie less to each other when they are face to face and more when, for example, they send text messages. Extroverts lie more than introverts, even when we allow for the fact that extroverts interact more socially. Men and women lie more or less equally, but women lie more often to avoid hurting other people's feelings, while men do it more to highlight their own brilliance. Last but not least, we lie less often to those we have a close relationship with, and we also find lying to them more disturbing.

The first chapter is devoted to a conceptual clarification of what we mean by 'lying'. To achieve this, we will take a closer look at the concepts of truth and truthfulness, and we will also delimit lying from its close relatives, truthiness and bullshit. Lying is understood as choosing to say something you believe to be untrue in a context where the person you are talking to has reason to assume that you are telling the truth. It is important for our further discussion that the most basic terms are given a fairly precise meaning. The next chapter deals with the different views on lying within philosophical ethics, and can be said, roughly, to conclude that lying is nearly always wrong – and this applies to so-called 'white lies' too – but it also concludes that there are special cases where lying can be defended. After that we turn to certain type of lies, namely the ones we tell ourselves. We humans are notorious self-deceivers, yet we seem to have an obligation to be honest with ourselves. Also, if you are the 'victim' of a comprehensive self-deception, if you are unable to be truthful to yourself, then it's unlikely you will manage to be truthful to others. If you cannot trust yourself, no one else can trust you.

Lying is generally wrong, but lying to your friends is especially wrong because you have built a special trusting relationship with them, and that is the topic of the following chapter. Friends have a stronger obligation to be truthful with each other than they do with 'acquaintances' or strangers. It also means you have an obligation to tell your friends uncomfortable truths about themselves. Most reflections on friendship and lying are also valid for relationships with a partner or spouse. If anything, the points in this case are especially applicable since we are most likely talking about an even stronger connection, where a breach of trust in the form of a lie can be experienced as a particularly serious betrayal.

From there, we take a leap from lying in our closest relationships to lying at a societal level, and look at lying's place in the political world. After a review of the most important philosophical contributions on the role that lying can or should play in politics, where thinkers such as Plato, Machiavelli, Hobbes, Weber and Arendt are discussed, we turn to real politics and discuss why politicians – with an emphasis on heads of state – lie and whether they have a morally acceptable reason to do so. At the end of the chapter, we discuss the political figure thought by many to completely overshadow all other liars: Donald Trump.

In the concluding chapter, I discuss how we should relate to lies: not just our own lies – where the obvious answer is that we should try to avoid it – but to the fact that other people lie. Most of us are not very good at exposing liars. 'Signs' of honesty and dishonesty are of little use. The most you can learn from studying these signs is how to become a better liar, not how to become a better lie detector. However, you are wise to mostly assume that people are telling the truth for the simple reason that in general they do. You will be fooled every now and then, but it is better to be fooled occasionally than to go through life with a chronic distrust of other people.

ONE

What Is Lying?

Truth and Truthfulness

You might think that you need a well-developed theory of truth in order to explain lying, since lying is often regarded as the opposite of truth. But you don't. The opposite of lying is not the truth, but *truthfulness*. In the everyday sense, to say what is meant by truth is fairly uncomplicated. When Arne Næss conducted a survey among ordinary people about their perceptions of truth, a fairly common answer among the housewives at Vettakollen in Oslo and the others he asked was that something is true if that's how it *is*.[1] This put them on a similar line to Aristotle when he defined 'truth' in *Meta-physics*: 'To say of what is that it is not, or of what is not that it is, is false, while to say of what is that it is, and of what is not that it is not, is true.'[2] The statement 'the snow is white' is true if, and only if, the snow really *is* white.

Such an understanding of truth seems reasonable, although it is perhaps not that enlightening, because the next question is of course about what we mean by saying something 'is' such-and-such and what possibilities we have of being able to determine whether it is indeed such-and-such. We feel a need for something more, a 'deeper' explanation of what truth really is. There are myriad philosophical theories, developed over several millennia, all trying to explain the essence of truth. However, there is little evidence that we are any closer to a satisfactory answer today than we were 2,500 years ago. One example of these theories is that truth can be understood as correspondence between a statement and the facts; another is that a statement is true if it fits into a comprehensive whole of statements that we perceive to be true.

The difficulty in finding a satisfactory theory for truth is perhaps because looking for such a theory is doomed to failure. What all the usual theories on truth have in common is their assumption that truth has a core which can be found via a theory, or that the truth has a certain property that a theory can explain. However, a great deal suggests that the concept of 'truth' is so fundamental that we cannot explain it by referring to something deeper or *more* fundamental. To an extent I agree with a theory of truth, a so-called minimalistic one. A minimalist would say that if the matter concerns whether roughly 6 million Jews were murdered by the Nazis, the truth is that they *were*. If the matter concerns whether humans have 46 chromosomes and potatoes 48, the truth is that they *do*. The minimalist claims that there is little more to say about the truth than that. Various matters can be judged on the basis of their specific criteria, but there is no 'deep' or 'exciting' quality here, one which is common to all these matters and can be said to comprise the 'essence of truth'. Perhaps settling for such a theory on truth is enough, because we all *know* what telling the truth about something means, namely that we tell it like it *is*.

The everyday understanding of truth is sufficient for our purpose. There are trivial truths like 'London is the capital of England,' '4 July is the u.s. Independence Day,' 'gold is heavier than water,' 'the Sun is bigger than the Moon' and '2 + 2 = 4'. No sensible person would doubt that these statements are true. We can say that statements like these are paradigmatic truths. We also tend to think that there are similar truths that we have not found, and perhaps never will. For example, we do not know who murdered Sweden's prime minister Olof Palme. Although the Swedish authorities have said who they believe was responsible for his murder, we think there is a truth about this that we could have discovered, so the claim 'X murdered Olof Palme' would have been true. It is more controversial to argue that there are moral or aesthetic truths of this kind, but that will not be pursued any further here.

Whether you are lying does not depend on whether what you say is true or false, but on whether you *believe* that what you are saying is true or false. If I read a news article which says that a person has been convicted of a crime and I pass on that information to you, but it then turns out that the journalist who reported on the case had accidentally omitted a 'not' when he wrote the piece, and should have actually said that the person had never been convicted of the crime, it is obvious that I am not lying to you even if what I am saying is untrue. So you can tell a lie without lying if you are confused about what is true yourself. For something to be a lie, there is no requirement that whatever you are saying has to be untrue – it is sufficient that you believe it to be untrue. If I say that the prime minister is having an extramarital affair with the leader of the main opposition party, and I am also certain that this is not the case, yet I want those around me to believe so, then it will be a lie even if, many years later, their respective memoirs show that they actually did have an affair. As a result we have true lies, because what is crucial to whether something is a lie is the person's perception of the matter they are talking about, and not the matter itself.

The opposite of lying is not the truth, but *truthfulness*. The British philosopher Bernard Williams stressed that sincerity and accuracy were the two virtues of truthfulness.[3] By sincerity we mean telling others how we have actually perceived something, and by accuracy we mean endeavouring to reveal how something actually is. Sincerity has little value if you have made no attempt to distinguish truth from untruth, and accuracy is of no use if you say something other than what you think is true. Only when you possess these two virtues can you be reliable. You can betray the truth in two ways: either by not striving for accuracy, or by being insincere.

If we start with accuracy, it is clear that what is considered a reasonable effort to ensure the reliability of our own beliefs depends on how much is at stake. If we were to strive for the greatest possible certainty in any matter, we would never get anywhere. To say much about anything would simply be too demanding. It is always possible to examine something a little more thoroughly, take a broader and deeper view, explore alternatives and so on. At some point, one must make a pragmatic choice that the evidence is sufficient. Among the trivialities of everyday life, it is not usually necessary to dig very deep or explore lots of alternatives. However, if you are going to convey a significant opinion or do something that is of any consequence for anyone else, the requirements will be stricter. If you have made no attempt to confirm the accuracy of your views, you do not have the moral right to have them, and certainly no right to demand the endorsement of others. Of course, the right to freedom of thought is fundamental, and we have no right to force anyone to hold something as true, but that is a legal question, and it does not free an individual from the moral responsibility of examining the accuracy of the opinions they have.

We must distinguish between *truthfulness* and *truthiness*. The term 'truthiness', which in 2005 was named Word of the Year by the American Dialect Society, was coined in its current sense by the American comedian Stephen Colbert to describe the rhetorical strategy that involves allowing your gut feeling to decide what is true rather than relying on established facts and logic. The wrong assumption is to conclude that something which seems or feels true really *is* true, without bothering to investigate the matter further. In this case truth value is determined not by objective facts, but by the speaker's emotions. The idea is that if something *feels* true, then it is true. The problem with this kind of approach is that it does not discern between something that is perceived as being true and something that actually *is* true. According to such a theory it would be impossible to be mistaken about anything. There would be no truth, just a variety of *truthy* beliefs. The possibility of making a mistake is crucial to being able to talk about truth at all. If we cannot distinguish between what seems true and what *is* true, we cannot possibly talk about anything being true. 'True' will become a meaningless expression.

However, we can never be sure that what we believe to be true actually is true. What we perceive as true is therefore something that is always provisional. The truth is *evidence-transcendent*, which means that truth is always, in principle, beyond the evidence we possess in order to claim something. To put it another way: no matter how good our reasons are for holding something to be true, there will always be room for error. We can never be completely sure if anything that we hold true is in fact true. We must therefore always allow for the possibility that we have made a mistake, and keep searching for new truths. Only then can I really be said to have acted responsibly and maturely as a truth-seeker. We can never rest on our laurels, because what seems self-evident today might appear a hopeless delusion tomorrow. So does this mean that we never move closer to the truth about the world? That would be an exaggeration. Although we can never know if we have found the ultimate truth about anything, we are at least continually putting some mistakes behind us.

The German philosopher Immanuel Kant describes the idea of enlightenment as imperative to using one's *understanding* to transcend one's 'self-incurred immaturity':

> *Enlightenment is man's release from his self-incurred immaturity. Immaturity* is the inability to use one's understanding without guidance from another. This immaturity is *self-incurred* when its cause is not lack of understanding, but lack of resolution and courage

to use it without the guidance of another. The motto of enlightenment is therefore: *Sapere aude!* 'Have courage to use your *own* understanding!'[4]

This does not mean that I should ignore what others have thought, but it does mean that I have to take responsibility not only for what I think and hold to be true and good, but for what I communicate to others. I never have control over the truth – it always transcends the *reasons* I may have for holding something as true – but I can have control over my own truth, over my own efforts to speak the truth or not.

The Essence of Lying

Clearly defining what a lie is can be difficult because it is often not an either/or, but more like something that comes in degrees, where there is no clear point at which someone is no longer just speaking misleadingly, but has started lying. You can find yourself venturing into the borderland of lies if everything you say is true, but you have omitted such crucial information that the overall picture has become untrue. Some philosophers, such as Kant, would argue that in such a case this is not a lie, but merely a deceptive statement, which he believes is not quite as bad as a lie.

I have stressed that one of the two virtues of truth is accuracy, and that accuracy should mean expressing things in a way that is not misleading. The crucial factor for considering whether something is a lie should not normally be limited to the specific wording. Even if what you say is true in a literal sense, it can still be false if the purpose of the statement is to make people believe something that is false. As we know, on the subject of his relationship with Monica Lewinsky, Bill Clinton stated: 'There is no improper relationship.' Taken quite literally, this was true, because he was not having a relationship with his intern at the precise moment he said these words, but the purpose of the statement was to make people believe that there had been no inappropriate relationship in the past either. When asked to elaborate on what he meant, he said: 'It means that there is not a sexual relationship, an improper sexual relationship, or any other kind of improper relationship.' The journalist asked a follow-up question: 'You had no sexual relationship with this young woman?' And Clinton replied again: 'There is not a sexual relationship; that is accurate.' By consistently choosing to reply in the present tense, to questions that were specifically about his past, Clinton's answers were in a literal sense true, but it is still reasonable to consider his statement a lie in that the purpose of the statement was to make people believe something that Clinton himself knew was untrue.

A statement cannot necessarily be regarded as a lie based purely on the literal meaning of the words – were that the case, using figures of speech like metaphors and irony would make you a persistent liar. Conversely, the fact that what you're saying is literally true doesn't necessarily mean that you're truthful. You can, however, insist that it isn't a lie simply because the statement is true based on its literal meaning, but you have very little to gain from that, because it would still be a form of linguistic deception and no more morally justifiable than lying.

If lying is understood as not telling the full and complete truth, then we rarely do anything *but* lie, since we can never tell the full and complete truth about anything. In principle, every phenomenon is inexhaustible – there is always more that can be said. It can be as trivial as responding to a question about what you've done at work that day, in which case you cannot list absolutely everything. If I'm giving an introductory lecture on Kant's theoretical philosophy, I need to omit a few details – many of them important – in order to have a chance of introducing the students to this complicated theory. However, I will often point out that it is actually a bit more complicated than the explanation I have given, but that my explanation is nevertheless precise and comprehensive enough for our purposes. If you are a doctor and recommend that a patient starts a particular treatment, you won't be able to explain *every* possible risk; you will have to be content with explaining the significant risks.

We only start moving in the direction of lying when our deliberate omissions make us present things differently to what we believe the case to be. It is then that the second of truth's two virtues, sincerity, comes into play – where there are seamless transitions between lies and what in politics is often called spin or strategic communication. Politicians normally offer such meticulously selected information that only the details supporting their positions will be included. Spin could also describe the closing arguments of a defence lawyer, who will put a biased emphasis on advocating for the defendant's innocence despite knowing that the picture is more complicated in reality.

The Norwegian Penal Code used to contain a provision that anyone who has by 'false representation' sought to influence people's voting could be punished with up to three years in prison, but it was repealed due to the section being dormant. Had the provision been strictly enforced, it would of course have meant that many politicians had been living dangerously. Election promises, however, seem to be a genre where what's said is only loosely binding. You might ask if voters can reasonably expect there to be much truth in the context of an election campaign. Nothing about an election campaign situation suggests any general acceptance that communicating deliberate untruths is legitimate. Using euphemisms and exaggerations is one thing, but outright lying is something else. If you can't be reasonably sure of keeping an election promise in the event of you being elected, you shouldn't make that promise – and you should definitely be held accountable if you have lied. In this context, it must still be accepted that voters are so used to politicians laying it on thick, or at least piling on election promises, that their expectation of there being any honesty is lower than usual, but blatant lying is still unacceptable.

Spin is undoubtedly misleading, but it still isn't lying. It is only lying when you say something to make people believe something other than what *you* believe is the case. Augustine defines lying as saying something contrary to what you believe with the intent to deceive.[5] In philosophical discussions about how lies should be defined, there is huge disagreement regarding whether an intention to mislead or deceive should be included in the definition. When we are explaining what a liar is, we typically imagine a person who deceives others by intentionally saying something other than what they believe is the case. Nevertheless, I believe that deception should not be included as part of the *definition* of lying, because some statements can quite obviously be lies, even though there has been no intention to actually deceive anyone.

If one assumes that a lie must be intended to deceive someone by making them believe that the facts differ from what they really are, it becomes difficult to handle cases where a person says something untrue, and knows that it is untrue, but also understands that virtually any recipient will themselves know that it is untrue. In short, there are lies that are so obvious that they have no intention of deceiving anyone. Let's say that I have a reputation for being a notorious kleptomaniac, and one day at work my colleague's wallet is stolen from her desk, which is next to mine, while she is momentarily away from her desk fetching a printout. Not only that, it actually *is* me who stole it. When she asks me if I stole it, I deny it completely. I am therefore not telling the truth, and I'm aware that I'm doing so. Furthermore, aware of my tattered reputation in this particular area, I know that neither the owner of the wallet nor anyone else will believe me. So I have absolutely no chance of deceiving anyone by making them believe anything other than what actually happened – that I stole it. The only thing I can achieve by denying the theft is to avoid being punished, since proving my guilt won't be possible. In this situation, it would be obvious that I was lying, although with no intention for that lie to deceive anyone.

Another example could be the case of Mohammad Saeed al-Sahhaf, who became known as 'Comical Ali'. Al-Sahhaf was the information minister under Saddam Hussein and became famous for his daily press briefings during the invasion of Iraq in 2003, where he claimed, among other things, that there wasn't a single U.S. tank in Baghdad, even though any journalist present knew there were U.S. tanks just a few hundred metres away and the sound of fighting between American and Iraqi troops was clearly audible while he spoke. He couldn't possibly have believed that what he was saying was true, or that anyone would believe him. Yet his statements must of course be considered lies.

Such blatant lying, where there doesn't appear to be room for someone to intentionally deceive, can be considered an exceptional case of lying, and should therefore not be given too much importance in the further discussion. When I write about 'lies' without specifying what kind of lies they are, I'm referring to general 'normal' lies that also involve a deliberate effort to mislead or deceive. Both non-deceptive and deceptive lies break the rules of how we should communicate with each other, but the deceptive lies are more problematic because they also contain an element of coercion: the liar is attempting to deprive the recipient of the ability to make free and informed choices.

If I lied to you, I would normally try to mislead you in two areas: (1) about my state of mind, that is, what perceptions I have about a case; and (2) about the case itself. However, we can make a number of variations on this theme, where I can, for example, mislead someone by saying something that's true, but in such a way that the person I'm talking to will think that

I'm lying. Suppose I work in the stock market, and have my eye on a company that's about to be listed on the stock exchange. At the same time, one of my fiercest competitors is interested in the company too, but has very little reason to consider me reliable. If while talking to him I sing the company's praises, and even throw in a little fake enthusiasm, he will probably think I'm being dishonest and that I perhaps know something he doesn't. In short, that I'm attempting to fool him into buying big when the company goes public. The consequences of this could be that he decides against investing, while I make a killing. I would in this case be telling the truth, but misleading my competitor about my state of mind. Is that lying? Certainly not, for the simple reason that I would be saying something I actually believe is true. Another variation might be that I say something that both my interlocutor and I believe is false, but I say it in such a way that he thinks that I believe it to be true. Am I lying then? No doubt about it, even though my intention was only to mislead him about my state of mind, and not the actual facts.

The distinction between lying and general deception is more vague. I can lie without saying a word. If I know that my silence, in a given context, will be interpreted as me agreeing to something being true when I actually believe it to be untrue, I will be lying by remaining silent. Can I lie by laughing? Definitely not, but I can deceive with laughter if someone says something that is meant to be funny but isn't, and I laugh to avoid spoiling the atmosphere. The laughter, which in this case wouldn't be spontaneous but the forced kind, may not be a linguistic utterance, but by laughing I would be communicating the message: 'That was funny!' I remember once attending a dinner with a foreign ambassador where a famous Norwegian politician told not just one but several jokes at the table, none of which was funny. I think everyone at the table, except for the politician concerned, agreed. One of the jokes was: 'A boy and a girl were in love, and the boy said, "I love you!"

And the girl replied, "I love you too!" But the boy, not wanting to be outdone, said, "I love you three!"' An honest response to this would have been to look at the joker quite blankly, but that would have created a bad atmosphere. So was it right of me to laugh politely? Our laughter had reinforced the speaker's delusion that he is funny, which meant he would tell just as many unfunny jokes at the next dinner, where he would be met, once again, with false laughter. And so on. Luckily, I've never been to more than one dinner with him.

The story the joker had told concerned something that didn't happen. So was he lying when he told it? A lot of humour can be perceived as lying when taken literally. For example, if someone were to ask me how I want to die when that day finally comes, I could give them a straight answer, and say that to drift gently out of life in your sleep, when you're old and ready, sounds like a good way to go. However, I could also seize the opportunity to give my answer a funny twist, and say: 'I want to die in peace while I'm asleep, like my grandfather did, and not screaming in terror, like the passengers in the car he was driving.' There's not much truth in the latter statement. I don't know whether either of my grandfathers died while they were sleeping; they may have woken up just before it happened for all I know. But I do know that they were both in bed at the time, and that neither of them was behind the wheel of a car that dragged several other passengers to their doom. However, it should be obvious to most people that my answer was never meant to appear truthful, but as a joke, and that I am more like an actor when I say it. The statement's character, and the way I say it, should make it quite clear that it is not claiming to be true, and is therefore not a lie either.

However, not everyone has a well-formed sense of humour, and some will manage to take the statement literally. In which case, I'll of course swiftly clear up the misunderstanding. Some people also take most of what they hear literally, and are quite bad at handling figurative language. Sometimes we will say something that, if taken literally, is untrue, but which is mutually understood, and for that reason would not be lying. An obvious example of this is irony. For example, if I say, 'It's really nice weather today!' during a howling gale and pouring rain, I am normally being ironic. What I am saying is literally untrue because by most reasonable norms the weather isn't good at all, and I know that what I'm saying isn't true, but it is still not a lie. Within normal language, we have a number of techniques that enable us to diverge from literal meaning without becoming chronic liars.

I once received a furious email from a member of a tiny political party, accusing me of lying about the party. The background was that I had said, during a radio interview, that there was no one in Norwegian politics who spoke up for genuine *laissez faire*-capitalism – that is, that all economic transactions between private actors should happen without government intervention. I then added that the exception here was the Liberal People's Party, but I also pointed out that 'It has so few members, they would all fit into a phone box.' The furious email writer claimed that this was a blatant lie, since the party *did* have more members than could fit into a phone box, and, in a sense, my outraged critic was correct: the Norwegian record for the number of people who have squeezed into a phone box is twenty, and the Liberal People's Party had more than twenty members, which meant they would have needed to use several phone boxes. However, it was probably clear to most of those who heard the interview that I was not trying to say that the Liberal People's Party had fewer than twenty members, but merely pointing out that it was a tiny party with no influence in politics. When using rhetorical tropes – different figures of speech – you will normally be saying something that is not literally true. Nevertheless, it's quite obvious that you're not lying when expressing yourself like this because, first, you don't mean it literally, and second, it's normally clear that it should not be taken literally because of the context.

If you meet a slightly peripheral acquaintance who asks how you are, and you tell them you're doing great although strictly speaking you're actually not, it can hardly be called lying because the social convention here is about the exchange of standard phrases – it's more like a handshake than genuine communication. Breaking from those kinds of conventions can be quite strange, for example, if you ask a colleague how he's doing as you pass him in the corridor, and he responds by going into elaborate detail about the trouble his bleeding haemorrhoids are giving him. Most of us would sooner he replied 'good' instead, and since the convention for this type of communication is that we expect nothing but 'good' as a response, it's not lying if he actually says 'good' even if his life isn't exactly a bed of roses.

In contexts like this, we often don't regard what's being said as a genuine expression of what we think and feel. It is a ritual that must be performed a certain way. I can mean exactly what I say, or I can mean the exact opposite, but what I say in these situations gives virtually no indication of what I actually mean. It is precisely because the norms of politeness are so important in these situations that we cannot reasonably expect people to mean what they are saying, and that is why they are not lying if they say something other than what they mean.

Whether something is a lie or not will therefore depend on the context. Is it a situation where others have grounds to assume that you are being honest? In most situations they do. A clear example of the opposite would be when an actor is onstage, playing Ibsen's character Brand, for example. We wouldn't assume that the actor believes that a man's life should be devoted uncompromisingly to God, even if he is expressing that in his role onstage. The actor could be an atheist for all we know. In this context, the actor wouldn't be lying even if, while in character, he said something that he himself believes to be untrue, because the audience has no reason to expect the actor to be truthful.

What about novels? Is the fact that it says 'novel' on the book's title page enough to prove that its contents should not be seen as an expression of truth? It normally will. A case in doubt would be so-called 'reality fiction'. We can say that to the extent that a novel can be true, it can also be false. Kant would argue that a novel by definition cannot lie, for the simple reason that it cannot be true either. In his *Critique of Judgement*, Kant points out that fiction uses rhetorical means and creates an illusion, but that this does not imply any deception, because fiction has no pretensions to truth.[6] The art of fiction is therefore honest because it doesn't pretend to be true. The problem with reality fiction is that it does not dwell unambiguously in the realm of fiction. The reality effect that comes of using real and identifiable persons can undoubtedly have an aesthetic value, but the price you might have to pay for such a transgression of fiction towards reality is that you incur a responsibility to be truthful and the risk of being a liar.

Am I lying if I want to sell my car, and tell the prospective buyers that I will under no circumstances go below £20,000 when my real limit is £18,000? It depends on whether the negotiating of the price is a situation where there are reasonable grounds to expect truthfulness or if during the bidding rounds we are playing another language-game where truth is of no major importance. Obviously, I will be lying if I say something that I know isn't true about the car itself, for example, that it has only done 30,000 miles when in reality it has driven twice as far – on that point it would be reasonable for the buyer to expect the truth. But things are not quite as obvious when bargaining over the price.

Am I lying if I say something while believing that it's true, then find out that it was false, but do nothing to correct my previous statement? I wouldn't have been lying when I said it, because I had said what I believed was true; yet by remaining silent I would be helping to maintain a falsehood that I myself had put into circulation. This is surely no better than if I had lied in the first place. And of course, it is very serious if it affects a person's reputation, for example. Most of us have helped spread rumours, only to find out that they were quite untrue. The morally decent thing to do when this happens is inform those you spoke to that what you had said wasn't true. But few of us do that, presumably to avoid losing face.

The obligation to be truthful also applies to our activities on social media. Posting an article on social media is, in a way, recommending something, except for those cases where you also write something that problematizes the article. If you post it even though you don't believe it is true, but do it anyway because it will get you a lot of likes or harm someone that you don't like, then you are a liar. If you believe the article has some merit, and although it's done nothing to assure you of its veracity it has, for example, come from a credible source, then you are acting truthy. He who perpetuates a rumour is not a liar if he believes the rumour himself, although he is not being truthful, because it is unlikely he has done anything to be sufficiently certain that the rumours are true. In other words, if you want to be a reasonably truthful person you should be very careful about spreading rumours. The truth is that most of the news items shared on social media have never been read by the person doing the sharing; most people are usually content with reading the headline, and won't even bother to check that the headline is a fair representation of the article's content. It's surprising how often they don't, since a headline's primary function is to generate clicks. Even fewer bother to check if the article comes from a reliable source or if there's anything that supports the article's claims. To share an article is to put a stamp of approval on it, unless you are explicitly pointing out something else – and that means failing as a responsible participant in the public discourse.

Ludwig Wittgenstein writes: 'Lying is a language-game that needs to be learned like any other one.'[7] It is quite a strange assertion. When using language we are participating in various 'games' that have rules, but what exactly are the rules in the language-game of lying? All in all, lying is a tricky phenomenon to handle within the framework of Wittgenstein's philosophy. One of Wittgenstein's basic principles is that the understanding of internal processes always requires external criteria.[8] The question then becomes: what is the external criterion of a lie? It cannot be that a statement is untrue, because one can say something that is untrue without lying if one is confused about what's true. What separates the two is the specific *purpose* of the speaker, whether they want to hide what they are really thinking or not. How can this purpose *show itself* externally? The answer to that is anything but obvious. And as for lying as a specific language-game, it is more obvious to consider it a deliberate violation of the language-game's rules, just as a person who moves a rook diagonally on a chessboard would be breaking the rules of chess.

On the other hand, lying clearly has to be learned. Developing the judgement required to become a skilled liar takes practice. For example, you need to be able to say something relevant and credible. Let's say I have a long-running feud with one of my neighbours, who is then found dead, still warm, with a kitchen knife in his back, and the police ask me where I've been that day. I couldn't say that I've been in Antarctica, since that obviously wouldn't be true. Nor could I say that I've been in the northern hemisphere, because although that might be true, it would be so imprecise that it would just seem like an attempt to avoid answering the question. Neither would it work to reply that I believe that the COVID-19 pandemic will have lasting and serious economic consequences, because even if I believe this to be true myself, it is completely irrelevant. All three answers would be attempts to avoid replying truthfully to the question I'm being asked. The first of the three answers is a lie, although a bad one. The other two answers are true, but they are too imprecise or irrelevant. A functioning lie must appear true while misleading the police investigator in a purposeful way. It is an art that takes time to master.

One way to avoid blatantly lying is by using vagueness. The more precise wording I use, the more likely I am to say something untrue, and conversely, the more vague I am the higher the likelihood that what I'm saying is true. If I said that I weigh *exactly* 100 kilograms, it wouldn't be true. If, on the other hand, I said that I weigh *approximately* 100 kilograms, it would be. Suppose I'm invited to make a speech at a breakfast meeting. Since I don't like getting up too early, I'm quite tempted to decline. However, I have no other appointments that morning to prevent me from showing up, so if I say that I can't attend because I have another appointment, that will obviously be a lie. What I can do instead is be far more vague, and say that I unfortunately have other plans that morning, which is not such an outright lie since I *do* have a completely different plan for that morning, namely to sleep. It wouldn't be a significantly more honest answer, but it wouldn't be a lie.

So to gather the threads a little, we can determine that lying is to say something you do not think is true in a context where others can reasonably expect you to be telling the truth.

Bullshit

Before I leave the discussion about what lying is, and consider whether lying can be justified, we must briefly consider its close relative: bullshit. As we have seen, lying diverges from truthfulness by not fulfilling the virtue of sincerity, while truthiness diverges by not fulfilling the virtue of accuracy. Of the two, bullshit is more similar to lying than truthiness because what it lacks is sincerity. Bullshit, as with lying, is insincere, but it is perhaps characterized more as *ungenuine* than *untrue*. It is ungenuine because the speaker will act as if he or she is participating in an activity where it matters if something is true or false, but doesn't actually care either way personally.

In what follows, it will be the American philosopher Harry Frankfurt's analysis of bullshit that is used as a basis. An important forerunner of Frankfurt and his analysis of bullshit, which strangely enough is not mentioned in his essay, is George Orwell. In 1946 Orwell published the essay 'Politics and the English Language', in which he claimed that 'in our time, political speech and writing are largely the defence of the indefensible.'[9] There he showed, among other things, how the use of euphemisms and intentional vagueness broke down the meaning of political language. The theme was developed further in the novel *1984* (1949), where the main character, Winston Smith, who works in the so-called Ministry of Truth, says that most of what he dealt with is entirely disconnected from reality, even more than would have been the case with direct lies.[10]

For most people, including the liar, the fact that something is untrue is good reason for not saying it. For an accomplished bullshitter, on the other hand, it doesn't matter whether it is true or false. Both the liar and someone telling the truth claim to know what is true, while the bullshitter simply doesn't care. The difference between lying and bullshit is that the liar says something other than what the case is, while the bullshitter does not care at all what the case is. So what decides whether a person is lying or bullshitting is their attitude. It is about their indifference towards how something really is. Frankfurt writes:

> This is the crux of the distinction between him [the bullshitter] and the liar. Both he and the liar represent themselves falsely as endeavouring to communicate the truth. The success of each depends upon deceiving us about that. But the fact about himself that the liar hides is that he is attempting to lead us away from a correct apprehension of reality; we are not to know that he wants us to believe something he supposes to be false. The fact about himself that the bullshitter

31

hides, on the other hand, is that the truth-values of his statements are of no central interest to him; what we are not to understand is that his intention is neither to report the truth nor to conceal it. This does not mean that his speech is anarchically impulsive, but that the motive guiding and controlling it is unconcerned with how the things about which he speaks truly are.[11]

The bullshitter is only concerned with the *effect* of his or her statement, and so considers whether the statement is true or false to be irrelevant. So a statement can be true, yet still be bullshit. Normally bullshit is untrue, but sometimes a bullshit statement can be true: a stopped clock will show the correct time twice a day. According to Frankfurt, bullshit is a greater danger to society than lies, because it will 'undermine confidence in the value of disinterested efforts to determine what is true and what is false'. The liar is, after all, concerned with what is true, but says the opposite of what is true. It is analogous to double standards being preferable to no morals whatsoever.

Analytically, Frankfurt's distinction between truth, lies and bullshit is clear, but in practice it can be hard to determine what the speaker's intention is, and consequently into which category the speaker's statement falls. Furthermore, a statement that is essentially bullshit can also contain elements of lying, meaning that although the speaker does not initially care whether what he is saying is true or false, he also understands that parts of his claim are directly untrue. Conversely, a lie can also contain elements of bullshit.

The American philosopher G. A. Cohen argues that the essence of bullshit isn't found in the speaker's intention, but in the fact that what they are saying contains 'unclarifiable unclarity'; in other words, it is gibberish. We can say that Cohen regards bullshit as a purely semantic phenomenon. Here I am inclined to think that Frankfurt is more congruous with ordinary language than Cohen is, although the term is undoubtedly also used in Cohen's sense. If someone tells someone else that they are talking bullshit, it wouldn't normally be because they find what the person said incomprehensible, but because it is ungenuine. Normally a bullshit statement will be worded comprehensibly, but it is more intended to obfuscate a case than to state it. A truly dedicated bullshitter can word things in such a way that it is impossible to attribute any truth-value to his claim when you examine it more closely – it is a stream of euphony, beyond truth and untruth. It can still be totally understandable – just not very enlightening.

Determining if a person's false claims are lies, bullshit or truthiness can be difficult. Take the former u.s. president Donald Trump, for example. It is well documented that he makes false statements to an extent the world has rarely seen before. However, it is not obvious that he is lying. We have defined lies by referring to the speaker's beliefs, arguing that the speaker is saying something contrary to what he person-ally believes to be the case. It is conceivable that Trump has such a weak grip on reality that he personally believes in all the untruths he is presenting. If that is the case, then he is being truthy. Of course, it is also possible that he is well aware that what he is saying is untrue, in which case he is a liar. Or it could be that he does not care at all whether what he says is true or false, but is only concerned with the effect his statements have. In that case he is a bullshitter. To determine with certainty which category Trump falls into, we would need access to his inner world, which we don't have. We must therefore consider the matter more indirectly, based on how he behaves as a speaker. Of course, Trump also tells the truth now and then, but I can't think of a single case of him saying anything true that has been significantly detrimental to him. This suggests that he is not being truthy when he says something untrue, because you would then believe that there are cases of him saying things that were unfoundedly true that were not advantageous to him. Which leaves us with lies and bullshit. Of the two, all things considered, bullshit would appear to be a stronger candidate than lies simply because the truth appears to be totally irrelevant to him. However, it is totally conceivable that Trump really is interested in what is true and what is untrue, but consistently chooses to put consideration for himself ahead of consideration for the truth, which makes him a liar of epic proportions.

Truthfulness does not have one opposite, but three: truthiness, bullshit and lies. Our main focus here is to investigate the last of the three, but many of the troubling aspects of lying can also be attached to truthiness and bullshit, and will therefore be relevant to them as well.

TWO

The Ethics of Lying

Practically everyone agrees that in general, lying is wrong – even Machiavelli admits it – but some claim that lying is always wrong, while others claim that in some circumstances it's perhaps acceptable, a necessity even. Truth is the rule, lies are the exception. As the Swedish-American philosopher Sissela Bok points out, you don't need any justification for telling the truth, but you do need a reason to lie.[1] If you can achieve what you want by telling the truth – and unless you belong to the special group of pathological liars – you will simply prefer to be truthful than to lie. We therefore don't lie when the truth is unproblematic. Lying is something we resort to in order to solve a problem that the truth would create for us.

Some possible reasons for lying could be: (1) to hide the fact that we have done something wrong; (2) to help someone else who would have a problem if we told the truth; (3) to avoid hurting someone else's feelings; (4) to harm someone by, for example, spreading false rumours about them; (5) to appear better than we actually are; (6) to gain an advantage for our-selves; and (7) to be funny by telling a 'tall tale' or by mocking someone. I'm not claiming this is an exhaustive list of all the motives we can have for lying, but it should cover most of them. The last reason on the list stands out because it is not about solving a problem but is motivated simply by a need to entertain. In addition to these seven reasons, we also have totally unmotivated lies, where someone lies for the sake of lying, although that takes us into the realm of pathological lying. Of the seven types, some forms will normally be considered milder than others. 'White' lies, told in order to spare others, are far more acceptable than 'black' lies that are meant to harm others – and there are many shades of grey between the two.

Even the biggest liar imaginable will tell the truth more often than they lie. Lying is only possible because there is an institution of truth. If we did not mostly tell the truth, it would not be possible to lie. So there is also a lack of symmetry between truth and lies: you don't normally have to explain why you are telling the truth, but a lie will have to be justified, even if only to yourself. Apart from special cases where telling the truth will have very negative consequences – for example if telling the truth would put someone's life in danger – the truth rarely needs any further justification; speaking the truth is enough in itself. It's always possible to find a justification for lying, but if the justification is to be truly convincing, one is usually required to be dishonest either with oneself or someone else.

Aristotle is often credited with being the first to point out the asymmetry between truth and lies, by saying that truth in itself is commendable and that falsehood in itself is low and contemptible.[2] Humans work at their best when they succeed in finding the middle ground between two extremes, he claims, but in terms of lies and truth, there is no middle ground between them – the middle ground is almost entirely in the area of truth. He first sets the truthful against the braggart and the hypocrite, who make themselves appear greater or less than they really are, respectively. The virtuous man who follows the mean 'is one who calls a thing by its own name, being truthful both in life and word, owning to what he has, and neither more nor less'.[3] Furthermore, he stresses that those who are genuinely truthful don't just speak the truth when something important is at stake. Instead it is a pervasive characteristic: 'For the man who loves truth, and is truthful where nothing is at stake, will still be more truthful where something is at stake; he will avoid falsehood as something base, seeing that he avoided it even for its own sake; and such a man is worthy of praise.'[4] Anyone who lies about small things or about things that don't concern the matter being discussed will also undermine their overall credibility because they cannot be trusted when talking about matters of importance.[5]

Of course, there are plenty of good reasons to lie. The question is, are they good *enough*? The strategy of those wanting to defend the practice of lying in various contexts has normally been to explain the lie away instead of defending the legitimacy of lying. Their argument is normally that even if a statement immediately appears to be a lie, because it concerns a speaker who is saying something contrary to what he believes is the case with the intention to mislead, the statement should still not be classed as a lie. An example of this is the Dutch lawyer and philosopher Hugo Grotius, who claims that you are not lying if you say something untrue to a person who himself is telling a lie.[6] As Grotius sees it, neither are you lying if you intentionally say something untrue to a child or a person with a serious mental illness, nor if you speak untruthfully to an enemy or a thief. According to Grotius, what all these recipients have in common is that they have no right to the truth; since they do not have this right, not telling them the truth does not amount to lying. Grotius believes that the right to truth is first of all dependent on having sufficiently developed judgement; and second, on being honest and respectable. Consequently, it is not lying to say something untrue to someone who has not yet acquired the right to truth, such as children, or people who have lost the right because of their own erroneous intentions and actions.

A more extreme variant of this kind of strategy is the Jesuits' theory of 'mental restriction' (*restrictio mentalis*). In

The Provincial Letters, the French philosopher Blaise Pascal wrote a savage critique of the Jesuits' casuistry, which he regarded as no more than a dishonest attempt to circumvent morality and the words of scripture. Here he discussed, among other things, the doctrine of mental restriction.[7] This doctrine claimed that it is not lying if, after saying something clear and distinct, which in isolation would be a lie, one chooses to add something internally or spoken so quietly that nobody can hear it, and this additional something changes the meaning so significantly that the wording as a whole is no longer untrue. For example, if I testified in court because I was accused of murdering a very annoying colleague, and I was asked if I had done so, I could reply loud and clear: 'I have not killed him,' and then to myself add 'today' or 'with poison,' since after all it was a year since I did it and I had actually used a hammer, not poison. This internal addition would then, according to the Jesuits' casuistry, mean that I hadn't lied despite the fact that the part of my statement that was audible to those present was untrue. The Jesuits considered mental restriction an acceptable extension of another principle they defended, namely that it is not lying if you use deliberately ambiguous wording and make others understand your words one way while you choose to interpret them as meaning something else. The doctrine of mental restriction went further in that you didn't even need to find pertinent ambiguities but could just finish the sentence in your head, and in doing so change the meaning completely without telling a lie.

But the Jesuits were not content with that either; they also argued that a promise was only binding if the person had intended to keep it when they made it. So, for example, you could say: 'I promise to do X,' and then add 'if I can be bothered' under your breath, and you would then be completely unbound to your promise. The explanatory strategies are unconvincing because they were developed specifically to perpetuate the notion that lying is inadmissible, while you are in effect lying, accomplishing the same thing as you would have done by lying directly – and you do so with very similar means. If lying is wrong because it is an abuse of language, it is unclear why mental reservation or any other deliberately misleading way of expressing yourself should be less immoral than lying. Language is also being misused in these cases, to give others a false impression of what someone is thinking. Pascal believed that such a practice was breathtakingly immoral, and most readers of *The Provincial Letters* agreed. It was all considered so scandalous that in 1679 Pope Innocent XI condemned the practice. In defence of the Jesuits, it should be mentioned that they initially claimed that this type of 'non-lying' was permitted only when justice was at stake: for example, if you would be saving a life or preventing something said in the confession box from being disclosed. It must be said, however, that the practice became considerably more widespread than that.

Part of the problem with an absolute rule where every single lie is forbidden is that it creates such an incentive to find loopholes that in practice one will lie while claiming that lying is unacceptable. This in itself seems deceitful or at least hypocritical. It is no coincidence that the Jesuits' explanatory strategies were developed within the framework of a Christian mindset that had zero tolerance for lying, although it should be pointed out that the Bible is by no means clear on whether lying is always wrong. Admittedly, one of the Ten Commandments seems to forbid lying, but this commandment has different interpretations; Luther understood it as forbidding the slander of his neighbour, while the Jewish tradition believed it was specifically about falsely testifying in court. It should also be conceded that overall the Bible refers negatively to lying, and most unambiguously in the New Testament where the Devil is referred to as 'the Father of Lies' (John 8:44). In the Old Testament, especially in the book of Exodus, lying seems perfectly fine as long as it's for the benefit of the Israelites.

So it would be correct to say that there is more than a little ambivalence towards lying in the Bible, and it is therefore unclear what kind of lying is acceptable and what kind isn't.

Augustine was a man who more than anyone strengthened a total ban on lying in general within Christian thinking. To say something contrary to what one is thinking with the intent to deceive could never be justified, even in the most extreme situations where lying might, for example, help save another person's life.[8] God gave people language so that they could share their thoughts with each other, and it is therefore a sin to instead use language to deceive others about one's thoughts. He writes about having sympathy for anyone who would lie to spare a sick and frail old man from knowing that his son is dead, since the burden of this knowledge would most likely take his life. Nevertheless, he claims that lying must be avoided in such cases too because even this kind of lie undermines the general sense of truth, it will make lying easier next time, and we will soon find ourselves swimming in a sea of lies. Even what appears to be the most kind-hearted lie will lead us astray. However, he added that it is easier to *forgive* such lies, and that one can praise the good intentions of a person who has lied for such a reason, but one can never praise the lie itself. Thomas Aquinas agreed with Augustine that every lie is a sin – he believed that lies told out of good will or as a joke were less serious sins, but that they were sins nonetheless.[9] Telling a lie to harm someone was considered a mortal sin. Using language to mask the truth, rather than lying, wasn't considered so bad.

People did of course experience situations where telling the truth was, to put it mildly, problematic, because the consequences for themselves or others seemed unacceptable. And since disregarding the religious ban on lying was also out of the question, the solution was to try and avoid it instead. The problem with making loopholes is that it is so tempting to expand them, little by little, with each new situation that makes respecting the general rule against lying a problem.

Duties and Consequences

Immanuel Kant upholds the Christian ban on lying, but for a completely different reason. Kant states that we have a duty to be truthful.[10] By lying, he means saying something that is untrue with the intention of having it believed to be true. That the intention is for others to believe something to be true is an important distinction, because without this intention it is not lying, even if what's said is untrue. Kant therefore believes that pleasantries and the like are not lies, even if you don't mean what you are saying, because no one expects you to be honest when saying such things.[11] Jokes and tall tales are not lies either, even though they are untrue, if there is good reason to assume that the listener is not being led to believe that they are true.[12] Kant also rejects the idea of white lies, because they would either be so white that they don't violate any obligation, in which case they are not lies even if what you are saying is untrue; or they *are* violating an obligation, in which case the lie is by definition not white.[13]

Kant believes that we are not always obliged to convey our innermost thoughts. If we always said exactly what we were thinking, we would find each other unbearable. The human community requires a degree of pretence, 'a nice quality that does not fail to progress gradually from *dissimulation* to *deception* and finally to *lying*.'[14] At the same time, this is a transition from what is morally acceptable to what is not acceptable at all. Dissimulation is not very problematic because no one else has a right to hear our thoughts. The deception ends up in a kind of halfway category, where some forms of deception are acceptable while others are not. Kant is no stranger to the idea that it can be morally acceptable to mislead others. For example, in a lecture on ethics he says that you can pack your suitcases to make someone think you are going away even if you have no intention of doing so, but lying to them about having travel plans would be immoral.[15] You can refuse to answer or you can let people make false assumptions, but you cannot lie, no matter what.

Kant also believes that you can lie to yourself, to your 'internal judge', about having behaved more respectably than you actually have.[16] We have a duty to be honest with ourselves, and we deserve censure when we are not. Furthermore, he believes that by lying to yourself you become more predisposed to lie to those around you. If I am able to be honest with myself, I should also be able to be honest with others. By lying, I am not only failing others but myself, because I am making myself a worse person than I should be. Kant goes so far as to say that by lying I am annihilating my human dignity.[17] This may be an overly dramatic formulation, but that your respect or esteem for a person declines significantly when you find out that they are lying shouldn't be controversial.

For a liberal thinker like Kant, the distinction between law and morality is absolutely crucial. The parameters of law should extend far beyond those of morality, and being immoral should be legally permitted. Kant warns against legalizing morality because it would deprive people of the chance to act truly morally. In accordance with this, a distinction must be made between lies that are solely framed by the prohibitions of morality and those that are also framed by law.[18] Kant therefore distinguishes between ethical and legal lies, the difference being that a lie must cause someone harm for it to be a legal lie. What's precisely meant by 'harm' is for a person to be deprived of something that is rightfully theirs, such as an object or a service that someone has agreed to perform. To spread false rumours about someone can also be deemed relevant harm. In other words, Kant believes that you can legally lie as much as you want, except in special cases that concern entering into a contract, defamation and the like, but morally it is always wrong to lie. Kant also has a third category of lies that falls between the first two, lies that don't harm a particular human, but humanity itself.[19] An underlying premise here is that man is a social creature, and by lying I undermine the conditions required for society to arise and exist. More specifically, I undermine the trust required for people to live as a social group.

For Kant, an action is right if and only if it satisfies the requirements of one or more overriding principles that are valid no matter what the consequences of acting in accordance with them might be. An action is not considered moral or immoral because of the consequences it has, but because of the *type* of action it is. If I tell a lie, it will be an immoral act no matter how good the consequences of that lie are. It wouldn't be wrong because lying generally has negative consequences, but because lying in itself is immoral. It is not something that can be added to a calculation and potentially offset by good consequences.

That lies are wrong almost immediately follows the two most well-known formulations of the so-called 'categorical imperative':

1 Act only according to that maxim through which you can at the same time will that it become a universal law.[20]

2 So act that you use humanity, in your own person as well as in the person of any other, always at the same time as an end, never merely as a means.[21]

Based on the first, the so-called Formula of Universal Law, Kant states that morality must be strictly general, which means that you cannot make exceptions for yourself or anyone else. In fact you should only act in a given way if you can imagine *everyone* acting that way. Let us now take the maxim: 'You can lie if it is to your advantage.' Can this maxim be generalized? No, because it would destroy itself. If everyone lied to improve their own situation we would stop believing each other, and if we stop believing each other it will no longer be possible to lie. In other words, a world where everyone lies to each other becomes a world where no lie can succeed because nobody believes anything anyway. Lying is only possible if there is an institution of truth; in other words, that we mostly speak the truth. Reason therefore tells us that we cannot lie because only truthfulness can be thought of as an entirely general precept.

By the way, Kant's points are anticipated by Baruch de Spinoza in his *Ethics*, in which Spinoza writes: 'A free man never acts deceitfully, but always with good faith.'[22] A premise here is that a free human being is always rational, and if a free human being wanted to lie or deceive in any other way, they would have to do so because it is rational. If this were the case, we would have to assume that rational people always lie and deceive, but Spinoza dismisses that as absurd. He then raises the objection that lying must be rational if one's life can be saved that way, but counters that if reason were to command one person to lie, it would have to command all people to lie. However, that would be like saying that reason should command people to not have common laws, join forces and live in peace, which he again rejects as absurd.

When it comes to the second formulation of the categorical imperative, which states that one should never treat others only as means, but always as ends in themselves, we must first clarify what is meant by 'an end'. To be an end is to have the ability to formulate one's own purpose in life, to make a life plan and to choose to live one way instead of another. No other animal has this ability, which is why it is so crucial to human dignity itself. Now, we cannot escape the fact that we often have to use other people as a means, such as when we ask a plumber to come and repair some leaky pipes. But the point is that we should never reduce others to being exclusively something we can use at our own discretion. We would then be lacking respect for the human dignity of the other person.

You must respect other people's right to shape their lives. If you lie, you are not doing that. Lying to someone is therefore a paradigmatic example of treating someone as a means. Someone who tells you a lie is trying to make you believe that things are different to how they really are. By doing so the person in question is trying to gain power over you, since your perceptions must conform to his intentions rather than to the case itself. One could say that the lie deprives you of the ability to act freely.

Lying is a breach of the contract in which we regard each other as free and equal. The most fundamental intuition behind the Kantian ban on lying is that lying is a form of coercion. Where knowledge gives power, he who is deceived is deprived of power. The lie transfers power to the liar from the person who believes the lie. If I succeed in my intention to lie to you, your thoughts will be directed according to my will rather than an independent reality. The lie deprives you of real choices of action, and can give you other goals and prompt the use of different means than those you would have chosen otherwise. You may well end up with a better result than you would otherwise have had – even one that, in the clear light of reflection, you think is the best imaginable – but I have equally deprived you of the opportunity to make a free and informed choice about which way to go. Even the most charitable lie, motivated entirely out of consideration for someone else's best interests, is still a lie.

Kant wrote an article claiming that the duty not to lie has such absolute validity that even lying to save another person's life cannot be allowed.[23] As we have seen, Augustine shared a similar view, although for theological reasons; Kant's justification is secular. Kant's article was a response to a pamphlet by the French philosopher Benjamin Constant in which he attacked an unnamed 'German philosopher' who was obviously Kant. Constant argues that no one has the right to hear the truth if it leads to significant harm, for example, if a murderer demands to know the whereabouts of his intended victim. Kant does not accept this argument, stating that nobody has the right to lie out of human kindness. He claims that if someone is hiding in your house to escape a murderer, and the murderer then knocks on the door and asks if his victim happens to be with you, you have no right to lie. You can refuse to answer or slam the door, but you cannot lie. Kant claims that if you tell the truth you cannot be blamed for what happens next, for what the murderer might do with that information. You would have done as you should, and any subsequent course of events would be out of your hands. If, on the other hand, you lied, he writes that you would be complicit in any subsequent course of events.[24] For example, you might believe that the victim is hiding in your closet, while telling the murderer that his victim has snuck out through the back door and run into town. Then it could turn out that the victim actually *had* run into town without you knowing, which results in the killer finding his victim anyway. This would mean that your lie put the killer on the right track, and according to Kant it would make you complicit in the victim's demise, even if your intention was to help.

Kant's perspective may appear to imply that we should give more consideration to the killer than his victim, but that is not the case. Kant stresses that no harm is being done to the *murderer* by lying because the murderer is asking for information to which he has no legitimate claim. So one would think that there is nothing wrong with lying to him. However, Kant claims that by lying you are not doing something wrong to a single person, but to *all* people.[25] You are not violating the murderer's right to truth by lying to him, but you are violating humanity's right that you behave honestly by undermining the trust people depend on having with each other. It is not a very convincing argument as it stands. As for trust, we could also say that we should be able to trust that others will help us if we are in desperate need.

Other solutions to the problem could also be appropriate. What if Kant had given the killer the following answer: '*Er isst nicht hier*?' This would be a cunning response because it is pronounced exactly the same as: '*Er ist nicht hier.*' The first sentence means, 'He is not eating here,' and the second means, 'He is not here.' As long as you hadn't given the victim anything to eat, you would be telling the truth by saying that he is not eating there, but the point is of course for the murderer to understand the statement to mean that the victim is not with you at all. Kant would never approve of a solution like this, since using the audible similarity between the words '*isst*' and '*ist*' with the intention of misleading the killer would be tantamount to lying.

Bernard Williams claims that people like the killer in Kant's example do not *deserve* the truth.[26] It is quite a strange formulation. Is truth something we must deserve, and something we deserve in some situations and not in others? It would seem more reasonable to say that we have a right to the truth, and we have this right because in normal situations when we say something to someone, we are implicitly making a promise, specifically a promise to tell the truth. The idea that there is a right to truth, which is a result of the situation in which the communication occurs, seems more reasonable than truth being something that must be deserved, not least because the responsibility for deserving something lies with the recipient – who must make themselves worthy of it – while in terms of it being a right, it is assumed that the speaker is giving the recipient that right by communicating with him. On a normal day, we will interact with people we have never spoken to before, many of whom we will never speak to again. Since we have never spoken to them before, they cannot be said to have 'deserved' that we tell them the truth – they have had no opportunity to earn such a thing during their relationship with us. Nevertheless, most people believe that we also have an obligation to tell strangers the truth, presumably because their right to the truth is not subject to it being deserved. Can such a right be restricted? For example, we normally have a right to not be harmed by someone else, but this right can be limited by someone else's right to self-defence. I have the right to harm you in self-defence if you wrongfully attempt to harm me. I can also harm you in order to prevent you from wrongfully attempting to harm someone else. It wouldn't seem unreasonable to claim something similar about lying.

Personally, I'm inclined to agree with Bernard Williams that not only would lying to this murderer be right, but nobody lying for such a reason should feel the tiniest shred of guilt for doing so.[27] Anyone who loses a wink of sleep for telling such a lie has had some kind of moral malfunction. He would not, to use Aristotle's description, be feeling what's right, in the right manner, at the right time.

Arthur Schopenhauer basically follows Kant's thinking, and claims that lying is a morally reprehensible way of forcing someone to serve another person's will.[28] He actually believes that lying is a worse means than violence because it destroys the bond of honesty that binds people together. However, unlike Kant, he believes that there are cases where lying is justified. These are, among other things, when doing so to safeguard your life and health, but he stresses that lying is also permitted when someone pries into your personal life and asks questions about things that are none of their business. He justifies the latter by saying that people should have enough understanding of social conventions to know that they cannot expect an honest answer if they ask inappropriate questions.

Kant's theory provides good reasons for why lying in general is wrong, but it handles some of the exceptions poorly. It fails to consider the uniqueness of some individual cases, and so ends up treating all cases equally when evaluating them differently would show better moral judgement. Kant's analysis is also not adequately sensitive to context, to how people can have good or bad reasons for lying. And as we will see in a later chapter on lying and politics, there are good reasons to believe that in some cases lying is not only permissible, but a necessity.

From a consequentialist standpoint, the murderer example seems quite unproblematic: since the consequences of lying are clearly better than telling the truth – because the gain is saving a life while the cost is only telling a lie – one should obviously lie. The consequentialist ethic simply states that one must always act in a way that will produce the best possible consequences. From this point of view, no action is inherently good. Whether an action is good depends entirely on its consequences. Similarly, no action is inherently bad, and any action can be good if its consequences are better than the alternatives. So from that perspective, truthfulness has no more positive value, in principle, than lying – whether one or the other is preferable is dependent on the consequences.

It should be emphasized that this refers to the consequences for all those affected. That something benefits you personally is all well and good, but your needs are no more important than anyone else's. If the consequences of a lie are good for you, but bad for others, we need to look at the results as a whole. The British philosopher Jeremy Bentham introduced the principle that for an action to be good it must bring the greatest happiness to the greatest number of people.[29] An action should therefore be carried out if it creates greater happiness – or it prevents more suffering – than the alternative actions. It is an impartial principle: every person's happiness is of equal importance in the utility calculus, whether they are a beggar or prime minister. As Bentham puts it, each person should count for one, and none for more than one. This doesn't mean that everybody will be afforded the same amount of happiness. What's crucial is *the total sum* of that happiness. If the total sum of happiness is likely to be greatest if some people are given an extremely unhappy role, which is however more than compensated for by the surplus of pleasure the other people receive, then it is morally right to give those few people the unhappy role.

So it may be right to lie to someone or, for that matter, spread false rumours about someone else if the consequences of doing so are better than not doing so. In that sense, the consequentialist ethic seems to throw the door wide open to lying. But that is not the case. Although the consequentialist ethic does not claim that lying is inherently wrong, for the simple reason that it does not claim that *anything* is inherently wrong, it ultimately concludes that practically speaking it is always wrong to lie. The main reason for this is that it is undoubtedly beneficial to have an institution of truth. If we were unable to trust each other, social interaction would be extremely demanding. It is also hard to evaluate the consequences of a lie, and evaluating the long-term advantages and disadvantages of a lie is even more problematic, even if the immediate benefit is significant.

John Stuart Mill, who developed Bentham's consequentialist ethic further, writes: 'A lie is *wrong,* because its effect is to mislead, and because it tends to destroy the confidence of man in man; it is also *mean,* because it is cowardly – because it proceeds from not daring to face the consequences of telling the truth – or at best is evidence of want of that *power* to compass our ends by straightforward means.'[30] In general, Mill regards our sense of truth as one of our greatest strengths, and everything that weakens it as fundamentally evil. However, he says that there are exceptions to this, and that a primary task for a consequentialist ethic should be to demonstrate how one can take into account consideration for upholding the truth on the one hand while preventing certain evils on the other.[31] He warns that this rationale can easily get out of hand, so one should therefore be very reluctant to lie. Mill adds that if the only way you can praise someone is by lying, then you should not praise them.[32] He also rejects the use of allegedly white lies.

When we lie in our everyday lives it is largely because we believe that the consequences of that lie require us to; that usually means the consequences for ourselves, of course. We often put too much emphasis on the immediate consequences – to save ourselves from an embarrassing situation or avoid hurting someone's feelings – and too little emphasis on the long-term consequences for both our relationship with the person being lied to and the institution of truth in general. This also applies to seemingly insignificant lies. Most of us have had friends or acquaintances who repeatedly told little lies, maybe about something as trivial as why they came late to an appointment or didn't show up at all. In these cases, the lying will sometimes become so routine that you simply cannot trust them. I have no friends like this – apart from those who *were* friends of mine and have been 'relegated' to mere acquaintances.

Lying is only possible on the condition that, by and large, we trust each other. This trust is a prerequisite for a society to function at all or even exist. A lie is a betrayal of this trust. However, lying will not always undermine trust. If you have a secret that I know about and you are afraid of this secret being revealed, and I then lie in order to keep your secret, your trust in me will probably increase. Conversely, if I refuse to lie and consequently reveal your secret, your trust in me will be diminished because you will realize that your interests are of only very limited importance to me. So there are situations where lying can promote interpersonal trust and where being truthful can weaken it, but it is usually the opposite way round.

If someone lies, it's not as though our relationships with each other promptly fall apart – and that societal collapse is sure to follow – but every single lie contributes a little. There are cases where telling the truth will have such bad conse-quences that lying seems to be a lesser evil. Would I have lied to save the life of an innocent person? Undoubtedly. Have I ever been in that situation? Definitely not. As Sissela Bok points out, there is something questionable about using examples such as 'lying to save someone from a crazy murderer' to argue that it is sometimes necessary to lie, because it is a situation that doesn't occur in most people's lives, and should it occur, it rarely happens more than once.[33] In short, the situation is so extraordinary that it doesn't give us a significant basis for saying anything more general about the need for us to lie. I don't think I can come up with a single case during my fifty years on Earth where lying has been necessary because the consequences of telling the truth would have been catastrophic. As such, I should probably conclude that not one of the lies I have ever told has been morally acceptable. Or is there a type of lying that is right, even in less dramatic circumstances?

White Lies

Is there such a thing as a white lie? What exactly is a white lie? As we have seen, Kant rejected the expression itself because it either had to be something so white that it could not be called a lie or something that had to be a genuine lie, in which case it could never be called white. There is no clear consensus in the literature on exactly what the term should mean. White can mean 'harmless', 'insignificant', 'charitable' or 'acceptable'. Can a lie ever be white if it is told primarily for your own sake? If it is fairly insignificant, perhaps: for example, if I were to offer a short, untrue reason why I couldn't go to the cinema instead of a far more long-winded, but true, explanation. Some people use the term in a broader sense about lies that have positive consequences and are, for example, used as a means of self-defence despite the fact that they can also have serious consequences for some and are therefore not 'harmless'. The distinction between white and black lies is not clear. It doesn't quite seem to fully coincide with the distinction between good and bad consequences, justice and injustice, good and bad intentions, altruism and egotism and so on, although all these things may influence our evaluation of whether a lie is white or black. There is hardly any clear distinction anywhere between white and black lies; there is instead a gradual transition from white to black, filled with numerous shades of grey. Most often, 'white lies' seem to be used in the general sense of 'a lie told out of politeness, or to avoid hurting someone's feelings'.

Suppose that Laura, who is married to Francesco, has been having a long-standing affair with Francesco's best friend, and that she is lying about this to Francesco 'to avoid hurting his feelings'. Most people would think that Laura's lies are fairly black, even if – at least according to what Laura tells herself – they are motivated by her consideration of Francesco's feelings. Her lies amount to a massive deception, and they are without question harmful to Francesco since they deprive him of the opportunity to freely consider whether he actually wants to be married to a person of Laura's calibre. We must therefore be more specific and, for example, add that a lie can only be white if it does not harm anyone. Laura's lies would then fall outside this definition because they are harmful to Francesco. It is simply not true that what you don't know cannot hurt you. Her lying forces Francesco to remain in a relationship with someone who is very different to what he thinks. What if Laura ended the affair with Francesco's friend, and now sees it as a mere slip-up that shouldn't have consequences for her relationship with Francesco? Would lying then be acceptable? It should be up to the person deceived, not the person who cheated, to decide if this was just a little mistake that shouldn't have any consequences. The lie has deprived the person deceived of the opportunity to assess if the relationship is worth saving in light of what has happened. The liar may convince themselves that the lie was justified by their wish to spare their partner any injury, but a more independent view will of course see things far more clearly: this was less about selflessness than a fear of being confronted, of losing face and not least of losing a person who means something to Laura.

What if Laura keeps the lie going, and you know about it, but Francesco is a good friend of yours? You also know that Francesco would be pretty crushed to know about the cheating because so much of his identity and life purpose is built on their marriage. Do you have to tell him the truth? There is no general answer to the question, but you should at least not lie to him yourself in order to cover up Laura's lying. By lying, you would be depriving Francesco of the opportunity to build a different sense of purpose in life, without Laura, preferably one built on stable ground.

We should add one more requirement: the lie must be for the benefit of the person being lied to. For example, complimenting someone on their clothes or how they have decorated their home, when you actually think both are terrible. Or you might say that a meal tasted delicious, when the truth is that you struggled to stop yourself from gagging. Then again, perhaps the food was fine, but the dinner party itself was deadly boring, yet you still say how nice it was when you leave. All these cases are about sparing someone else's feelings, because it is assumed that they would be upset if you told them what you really meant. However, it cannot be ignored that often, when someone says they have told a white lie, the determining factor is not consideration for someone else's feelings, but a need to spare themselves the discomfort of telling the truth.

What about a doctor who believes that it is not in a patient's best interests for them to know the truth? For example, it could be a reassuring lie before surgery about the unlikelihood of complications during such an operation, when in reality there is a more significant risk. What if the doctor isn't an especially good liar, and the patient sees right through him? This could make the patient even more afraid. How would further treatment be affected if the patient feels he can't trust the doctor to tell him the truth? Suppose a doctor found that I only have a few months left to live, but that I will live fairly symptom-free as I approach my expiry date. The doctor might consider sparing me by not mentioning my impending demise, to allow me to live the rest of my allotted time reasonably untroubled. But by doing so, he would be depriving me of the opportunity to spend what little time I had left as I wished; given that it would soon be over, I may have wanted to straighten out whatever needed to be straightened out, do what needed to be done now, because it could no longer be postponed, and say my goodbyes to the world.

What about lying to someone on their deathbed? When it was clear that my father was nearing the end, we had several good and intimate conversations in which neither of us hid the fact that time was running out for him. I would have liked to have had those conversations with my mother too, but she absolutely refused to consider the possibility that she would soon die. I didn't lie to her by saying that everything would be fine; nor was it my job to confront her about her imminent death when she didn't want that.

The idea behind white lies is that they are harmless, that they literally do no harm to anyone. Is someone who wants to tell such a lie the right person to judge its innocence? First, the liar cannot be certain that the person being lied to would not have preferred to be told the truth. The white liar is somewhat arrogant because he assumes the other person would have been unable to cope with hearing the truth. By lying for compassionate reasons I am appointing myself judge of what you can handle knowing: about your own life, about your relationships with others and about your reputation. Second, the white liar overlooks the corrupting effect the lie has on his own moral character; that it makes it easier to tell the next white lie, and then progress to the more grey-coloured lies, until it becomes increasingly natural to start telling black lies too. White lies undermine the habit of truthfulness. Montaigne writes: 'Lying is an accursed vice. It is only our words which bind us together and make us human. If we realised the horror and weight of lying we would see that it is more worthy of the stake than other crimes.'[34] Burning liars on a bonfire is perhaps overreacting, but that lying undermines the interpersonal trust on which we are so dependent is indeed an important reason why lying is so morally problematic.

When you feel tempted to lie, you should try to put yourself in the other person's shoes. How would you feel being lied to in a similar situation? How would that change your view of the person lying to you? It might be something trivial, but if you were to discover a lie you would then know that here is a person who lies when it suits them, and your trust in them would be broken. It would change your view of that person. And if it happens again, your trust will be shattered again, and the relationship will inevitably deteriorate.

I once took a girlfriend along to a dinner party that was being hosted by an ambassador. She had never been invited to anything like it before and, feeling a little insecure, had asked for my advice on what to wear. I don't remember if my answer was too unclear or if she simply misunderstood, but when I met her shortly before the dinner began it was obvious that the dress she'd chosen was not appropriate for the occasion – it would have been better had it come a lot closer to reaching her knees. But with the dinner about to start there was no time to swap the dress for anything else, so I just told her that she looked nice, and felt like I was making the best of a slightly tricky situation. In retrospect, I'm not at all sure if this was the right thing for me to do. Without us ever talking about it later, both she and I clearly noticed the other guests reacting to her dress, although nothing was actually said, of course. My white lie did nothing to alleviate her nervousness. It perhaps even reduced her confidence in trusting me on future occasions. Not least, I had denied her the opportunity to take responsibility, by assuming that she would be unable to cope with hearing that the dress was too short. What I did was with the best intentions at that moment, but I doubt if the consequences were very good in the long run.

It is often more tempting to be encouraging than to be honest because it creates a better atmosphere. Sometimes philosophy students will ask whether I think they should pursue the subject further, and the easiest thing for me is to answer encouragingly. The student will get the answer he or she wants, and my department will increase its revenue. But I always try to answer these questions as honestly as possible, and base my answer on whether I believe the student has any particular talent for philosophy. Such talent isn't clearly correlated with exam results; there are students who are 'good', and get good grades, but the chance of them developing into something more than just 'good' seems unlikely; and there are students who are undisciplined, who don't do things quite by the book and for whom getting top grades is less relevant, but who may demonstrate through discussion an exceptional capacity for philosophical reflection. So I have told students with fairly good results that they should perhaps find another subject, and I have told students with somewhat mediocre grades that there might be a future for them in the field, provided their work becomes more disciplined. Were I to tell a 'good' student, who I don't believe will go especially far, that the future is so bright they'll be needing sunglasses, simply to avoid hurting that student's feelings, it would be a white lie. It would not, however, be a lie that would benefit the student in the long run.

If I lie to you, then I am blocking your access to reality – and this applies to both white and black lies. By doing so, I am depriving you of your freedom. No matter how much goodwill my white lie is based on, I am denying you an insight you could have gained from your surroundings or from yourself. The truth could have set you free. It could have revealed how you need to change something in your life. The truth can also have painful or even destructive consequences for you, but it would be arrogant of me to assume that the truth is more than you can bear.

Adam Smith claims that even someone whose lying does no harm, who lies with the best intentions to promote someone else's well-being, will experience a degree of shame, remorse and self-condemnation.[35] I'm not convinced that he's right about lies always being accompanied by such pangs of conscience, although they should be. Of course, white lies are less upsetting than grey and black ones, because their purposes are more noble and they rarely have major implications, but they are still lies, and should be avoided.

Of course, saying that white lies should be avoided doesn't mean you should always dish out copious amounts of honesty. Staying quiet can often be an excellent alternative too. It's not always necessary to offer your opinion on something, and sometimes one can be a little too brutal when telling the truth. As William Blake points out:

> A truth that's told with bad intent
> Beats all the lies you can invent.

You don't always have to tell the whole truth. If someone hasn't requested your judgement, you are not duty-bound to offer it. They may have good reasons for not asking for it. On the other hand, if they *have* requested it, you won't help them by, for example, praising them for something that doesn't seem right. Just because what you are saying is true, that is not enough in itself to justify you saying it. Politeness is also a virtue.

THREE

Lying to Yourself

We normally think of a lie as something that transpires between two parties. But what if the sender and recipient of the lie are one and the same person? Can you lie to yourself? And if you can, the next question must surely be, why would you do it?

It's conceivable that self-deception exists because it improves one's ability to deceive others. If I can believe a falsehood myself, I stand a better chance of making others believe it too. I simply want to be more convincing. But that, of course, is just a hypothesis.[1] Nietzsche has given this some thought:

> With all great deceivers there is a noteworthy occurrence to which they owe their power. In the actual act of deception, with all its preparations, its enthralling voice, expression and gesture, in the midst of the scenery designed to give it effect, they are overcome by *belief in themselves*: it is this which then speaks so miraculously and compellingly to those who surround them. The founders of religions are distinguished from these great deceivers by the fact that they never emerge from this state of self-deception: or very rarely they experience for once that moment of clarity when doubt overcomes them; usually, however, they comfort themselves by ascribing these moments of clarity to the evil antagonist. Self-deception has to exist if a

> grand *effect* is to be produced. For men believe in the
> truth of that which is plainly strongly believed.[2]

As mentioned, lying is difficult because you have to have two thoughts in your head at the same time; both how something really is *and* how it is in relation to the lie. But if you can start believing your own lies instead, you only need to have one thought in your head.

Self-deception doesn't have to be directly about yourself. It can also be about your partner being faithful when he or she actually hasn't been, and a sober look at the 'evidence' clearly suggests infidelity. Knowledge like this can be so painful to absorb that it is often more tempting to cling on to the illusion. This type of self-deception is also about yourself, although indirectly, since it relates to someone else's relationship to you. However, self-deception often works as a form of self-understanding, such as overestimating ourselves despite our better judgement. People can believe they have less chance of catching the flu than other people, even when they know that they are in fact statistically just as vulnerable. The majority of motorists believe they are more than averagely skilled at driving in traffic. In a widely publicized study, 94 per cent of the employees at an American university claimed they were better at teaching than their average colleague.[3] Not least, most people believe they are able to make a more accurate judgement of themselves than the average person can.[4] In all of these cases, many of the people in question must have been overestimating their abilities. There are some situations where it's possible for a majority to be greater than average. For example, the average number of arms, legs and eyes that people have is fewer than two, since there are people who have lost an arm, a leg or an eye, but most people will have both intact and nobody has three. So in this case the majority will have more than the average. On the other hand, the vast majority of university professors cannot have greater teaching skills than the average of their colleagues. Whether overestimating oneself like this constitutes self-deception is less clear. It's quite possible of course that most university professors have been told that they are exceptionally skilled, and that the delusion about their own brilliance as educators stems from that. But equally often, it will be something they have told themselves, which makes the label 'self-deception' more appropriate.

There is no consensus among philosophers that self-deception exists at all. However, from this point on I am going to assume that the phenomenon is real. Self-deception is ostensibly lying to yourself. Like the liar, the self-deceiver must have an idea of what he or she believes the truth to be, and then claim something other than that. The difference here is that a regular liar will say something false to someone else while a self-deceiver will say it to him- or herself. What makes self-deception such a difficult phenomenon to understand is that it is inherently paradoxical, because a person evidently has to both believe and not believe in one and the same thing. The deceiver and the deceived are one and the same person, and all this has to be accommodated within one consciousness. Nevertheless, it seems impossible to believe both *p* and *not-p*. There is less of a paradox if we instead construct it so that the self-deceiver has more reason to believe *p* because there is better evidence supporting it, and they are also aware of this, but since they have many other beliefs, they choose to ignore this evidence. Not only that, I may *want* the truth to be something in particular. So, for example, a member of a sect can continue to believe that the sect leader is an excellent person despite there being good reason to think otherwise. A mediocre artist can explain away why they have never made it big, even when it's clearly because they simply aren't good enough. Some people who feel lonely can explain why this is by claiming that everyone else falls short, instead of admitting that it's sometimes themselves who fall short when it comes to appreciating the relationships they do have with other people.

As already mentioned, Bernard Williams claims that truthfulness has two components: sincerity and accuracy. It is most natural to believe that the weak component is the self-deceiver's sincerity. However, Williams claims that it is more likely the second point; that the self-deceiver has failed him- or herself in terms of accuracy. Self-deceivers are sincere but fail to ensure that their sincerity isn't built on quicksand. Williams compares this with ordinary forms of deception, like a conman tricking someone into believing something errone-ous, and argues that in such cases it is just as important to counteract the defrauded person's tendency to be deceived as it is to combat the fraudster. In that sense, Williams seems to agree with Homer Simpson's response in an episode of *The Simpsons* when, after being caught lying by his wife, he says: 'Marge, it takes two to lie – one to lie and one to listen.' It is an attempt to argue that they are both responsible for the lie he has told, since Marge was also complicit by listening to him. A genuine exchange of information requires both the listener to be accurate and the speaker to be sincere. Williams contin-ues: 'If there is such a thing as self-deception, the same, surely, should apply to it; our failures as self-deceived are to be found more significantly, in fact, in our lack of epistemic prudence as victims than in our insincerity as perpetrators.'[5] Based on such an analysis, self-deception should be more closely related to truthiness than to lying.

It is perhaps more difficult to be truthful to oneself than to others. So-called self-insight tends to be more truthy than truthful. Pascal writes: 'It is no doubt an evil to be full of short-comings; but it is an even greater evil to be full of them and unwilling to recognise them, since this entails the further evil of deliberate self-delusion.'[6] Still, it would be hard to go through life without applying a fair amount of self-deception. If you were to redact every self-flattering embellishment from your life, the result would be more than a little disheartening. Perhaps we should try doing it anyway. Kant argues that we have an obligation to be honest, not only to others but to ourselves. Man is the only being capable of gaining insight into himself and has a duty to seek insight into himself, in order to become a *better* human being through doing so. Kant thinks there is reason to believe that most of us would reach a disconsolate conclusion were we to conduct a sober and sincere examination of ourselves. According to Kant, however, man has such a proclivity for self-deception that it's unusual for him to have any insight into how miserable he is. Nevertheless, self-deception is rarely so absolute that we don't acknowledge there is a distance between who we are and who we should be. But not everyone comes to that realization.

Rousseau's Uncompromising Self-Deception

The philosopher who perhaps most emphatically proclaimed that he should be ruthlessly honest, not least about himself, was Jean-Jacques Rousseau, although he turned out to be a notorious liar and probably lied most convincingly to himself.

In the two volumes of his *Confessions*, Rousseau claimed that his truthfulness was unsurpassed. He further surmised that there was no need to search beyond himself, that to reveal these truths he just needed to consult his emotions. Unfortunately, his *Confessions* are, to put it mildly, unreliable, something he even admits to in his final work, *Reveries of the Solitary Walker*, where he adds a deluge of new falsehoods to the old ones. Rousseau says that one particular lie he told in his youth, which had terrible consequences for an innocent chambermaid who was blamed for a theft that he actually committed, had troubled him greatly in hindsight. He writes: 'The memory of this unfortunate act and the inextinguishable regrets it left me have inspired in me a horror for lying that should have preserved my heart from this vice for the rest of my life.'[7] It perhaps should have, but it certainly didn't.

The British philosopher David Hume, who was unfortunate enough to be Rousseau's friend for a while, said that he thought Rousseau really believed that he was telling the truth about himself, although in reality there was hardly anyone who knew themselves worse.[8] It's not hard to agree with Hume's verdict. *Reveries of the Solitary Walker* is a book largely devoted to paranoid fantasies about his enemies' malicious conspiracies against him, although it was Rousseau himself who ruined all his friendships by behaving like an asshole. He himself wrote that 'as for evil, my will has never been entertained by it, and I doubt if there is any man in the world who has really done less of it than I.'[9] Rousseau never managed to take a reasonably sober view of himself, and he therefore went through life without ever getting to know himself, despite the fact that he was uncompromisingly self-absorbed. Since Rousseau was incapable of being truthful to himself, he was also incapable of being truthful to others, and was therefore completely untrustworthy.

It is just a tiny bit ironic that Rousseau's life motto was: *Vitam impendere vero* ('To devote one's life to truth'). You could say he almost perfected the art of keeping life and learning apart. Rousseau wrote an influential work, *Émile*, about how children should be given a perfect upbringing, but chose to leave the five children that he had with his lifelong partner, Thérèse Levasseur, in an orphanage right after they were born. His justification for this was mainly that he couldn't afford to have children, and that it was out of consideration for Thérèse's honour, and that growing up in the orphanage would make the children more 'robust'.[10] The fact that the orphanage had a sky-high mortality rate, well above the average in France at the time, didn't seem to worry him. Admittedly he may not have realized quite how miserable conditions were at the orphanage, but there's no way he could have sincerely believed that it would offer them good conditions for growing up. Furthermore, he stresses that children brought up in this way could become ordinary workers or peasants, rather than living the kind of decadent society life he had lived himself. To give it more philosophical justification, he refers appreciatively to Plato's theory that the responsibility for bringing up all children should rest with the state and that no child should know its parents. It seems more like a series of rationalizations than honest statements. In *Confessions* Rousseau writes about how he, along with Thérèse's mother, managed to persuade Thérèse to give the children away because it was a quite normal thing to do, and that his actions didn't cause him the slightest anguish.[11]

The most obvious explanation for Rousseau choosing to put his children in an orphanage is that they were simply an obstacle to his self-realization – he wanted to continue living as he always had done. However, Rousseau is so convinced of his own excellence, his almost limitless compassion and goodness, that he never once considers that this might be so. As he writes in *Confessions*, he was in his own eyes, all things considered, the best of men.[12] Nevertheless he must surely have had some latent awareness that what he'd done wasn't acceptable. He describes a lunch where a pregnant woman asked him if he had children, and knowing full well the truth, 'Blushing up to my eyes, I replied that I had not had this good fortune.'[13] Obviously, he didn't feel that what he had done was unproblematic enough for him to talk freely about it.[14] He also admits to having lied many times out of shame to avoid embarrassing situations. How is that compatible with the claim that he has put the truth before everything else in life?

Rousseau addresses this issue himself, writing that he is amazed by how many lies he has told despite his unconditional love for the truth.[15] Not only that, he also stresses how he feels no remorse whatsoever for lying to save himself from embarrassing situations. To solve this problem, he resorts to all sorts of convolutions, such as claiming that it is only lying when the person you are speaking to might benefit from hearing the truth; since most of the falsehoods he had expressed were of the supposedly worthless kind, they couldn't be regarded as lies. This is a problematic criterion, because how can you be so certain about what might 'benefit' the person you are talking to? The criterion he uses is: 'From all these reflections, it follows that the commitment I made to truthfulness is founded more on feelings of uprightness and equity than on the reality of things, and that in practice I have more readily followed the moral dictates of my conscience than the abstract notions of the true and the false'.[16] In other words, something is only a lie if Rousseau's conscience tells him it is a lie. He seems to think that as long as his conscience is good, all is well.

Conscience is essential to self-knowledge, but it is not an infallible source of self-knowledge, as Rousseau believed. If you have done something wrong, you should have a bad conscience. But you can't conclude that you don't have a bad conscience and then say that you've done nothing wrong. An extreme example of this fallacy is the case of Lieutenant William L. Calley, who was the highest-ranking officer to be convicted for the My Lai massacre on 16 March 1968. Over the course of ninety minutes, 507 innocent people were murdered, including 173 children and 76 infants. Calley alone killed 102 people. The official report said: '128 enemy killed in battle.' First, 507 people were killed, not 128; second, they weren't killed in battle, but simply slaughtered; and third, they were not enemies, as in enemy soldiers, but ordinary civilians. In Calley's own eyes, he had only done what was expected of a good soldier, and he couldn't believe it when he was accused of mass murder:

> I couldn't understand it. I kept thinking, though. Could it be I did something wrong? I knew that war's wrong. Killing's wrong: I realized that. I had gone to a war, though. I had killed, but I knew – so did a million others. I sat there, and I couldn't find the key. I pictured the people of My Lai: the bodies, and they didn't bother me. I had found, I had closed with, I had

destroyed the Viet Cong: the mission that day. I thought, It couldn't be wrong or I'd have remorse about it.[17]

Conscience needs to be supplemented by a sober look at what one has actually done. Conscience alone gives you truthiness at best, not truthfulness. Conscience comes from the Latin *conscientia*, which is in turn synonymous with the Greek *syneidesis*. These words have something in common, something their prefixes (con- and syn-) testify to. The words allude to a co-knowledge, a knowledge of my own self. It is a matter of regarding ourselves and judging our own actions and motives. Self-deception prevents the ability of the conscience to guide us in our actions. If we look away from the bad sides of our character and actions, we also become less inclined to act morally and to right the wrongs we have committed. We are morally obliged to tell ourselves the truth about ourselves. To admit how bad you are is in many respects an initiation into who you are, and through doing so you can hope to create a basis for becoming a slightly more decent person. You then have a goal to reach for, even if there is every reason to believe that you will unfortunately fall short once again. A conscience that works like Rousseau's is simply unable to provide insight or correct the mistakes one has made in life. It does no more than assure you that everything is perfectly in order. A conscience that's not receptive to correction is not a source of self-awareness, but of self-deception.

Anyone relating to the truth as loosely as Rousseau did will most likely, over time, become lonely. This condition is also the main theme of *Reveries of the Solitary Walker*:

I am now alone on earth, no longer having any brother, neighbour, friend, or society other than myself. The most sociable and the most loving of humans has been proscribed from society by a unanimous agreement.

In the refinements of their hatred, they have sought the torment which would be cruelest to my sensitive soul and have violently broken all the ties which attached me to them.[18]

Rousseau wanted his character to be defined by his gaze alone – not someone else's. But it was this specific refusal to accept that an outsider's gaze had anything to offer that caused his own gaze to be systematically twisted into self-flattery.

One source of looking critically at yourself can actually come from yourself. Adam Smith developed a theory about the 'impartial spectator'. We are social beings, and Smith writes about how our fear of loneliness forces us to associate with others, even when, for example, we are ashamed and feel a need to escape other people's judgemental gaze.[19] He stresses that anyone who would grow up in solitude would never get to know themselves.[20] Those living in solitude will misjudge themselves, and overestimate both the good deeds they have done and the harm they have suffered.[21] We need the gaze of others. But the most important moral gaze is the one we have. For Smith, morality is based in the power of imagination, in our notion of how we appear from the outside, where we evaluate our actions from the perspective of an impartial spectator.

The impartial spectator teaches us about our own insignificance in the big picture, that we are not the centre of the universe. From the impartial spectator's point of view your self-interests are highly legitimate, but you also see that other people's interests are legitimate, which can require that you strive to ensure that their interests are catered for too. When you strive to promote your self-interest, you must, according to Smith, do it in such a way that you become a continually better version of yourself: where you not only appear good to others, but really are good, where you are not just 'loved' but 'lovely' – worthy of being loved.[22]

As Smith points out, however, thinking badly of ourselves is so uncomfortable that we prefer to look away from whatever might dictate that we should pass negative judgement on ourselves. He continues: 'This self-deceit, this fatal weakness of mankind, is the source of half the disorders of human life. If we saw ourselves in the light in which others see us, or in which they would see us if they knew all, a reformation would generally be unavoidable. We could not otherwise endure the sight.'[23]

Self-Presentation and Self-Deception

Few of us manage to show our cards to ourselves, let alone to anyone else. *Gnothi seauton* (Know thyself) was the inscription above the entrance to the Temple of Apollo at Delphi. Gaining self-knowledge can feel like an obligation you have to yourself. But self-knowledge doesn't come easily. We are all con artists, not just conning others but ourselves, and we gladly credit ourselves with considerably more morally superior motives than we actually have. After all, we rarely lie as convincingly as when we have to be totally honest with ourselves. Eventually we start believing our lies, unaware that they actually are lies until our stories start clashing. This is why it can be uncomfortable when people you know well in one setting turn up in another, because it can be hard getting the different stories you have about yourself to match. In such situations we will carry on regardless – hoping we are not revealed, either by ourselves or anyone else.

It might be easier to be truthful with someone else than with yourself, but perhaps you can only be truthful with others if you are truthful with yourself. Other people can only trust you if you are truthful with them, and you can only trust yourself if you are truthful with yourself. If you cannot trust yourself, no one else can trust you.

We are always managing our image. In 'The Love Song of J. Alfred Prufrock', T. S. Eliot writes: 'To prepare a face to meet the faces that you meet.'[24] We dress, for example, according to how we want to be perceived in different contexts. As social beings we play roles for each other while simultaneously monitoring ourselves to ensure that we play those roles correctly and comply with the social norms of the game. The Canadian sociologist Erving Goffman took this point so far as to claim that the self is just a set of roles that arise during social situations before an audience.[25] Without having to agree unreservedly with Goffman's socially reductive view of the self, it is clear that he captures something important. Not only do we create our own presentations about who we are, but we put on performances for others in which we play the role of ourselves.

Kant is positive about this because by playing such roles we can form good habits that eventually become a part of our moral character:

> Men are, one and all, actors – the more so the more civilised they are. They put on a show of affection, respect for others, modesty and disinterest without deceiving anyone, since it is generally understood that they are not sincere about it. And it is a very good thing that this happens in the world. For if men keep on playing these roles, the real virtues whose semblance they have merely been affecting for a long time are gradually aroused and pass into their attitude of will.[26]

Playing such roles does not involve deceiving anyone else, and we can become better people as a result. At the same time, we should be careful not to think too highly of ourselves, since there's no doubt that we have a tendency to do so.

A significant part of this involves making stories about ourselves for others, and this is where we can often be tempted to embellish the truth a little, or skip the more unflattering elements while magnifying others, or even invent things that never happened. We are all creative when making up stories about ourselves, and we cannot avoid making them. To have an identity is, among other things, to have a concept of your life as a story, where the past and the future give meaning to the present.[27] The story organizes your experiences into meaningful episodes and connects them to form a whole. In other words, we give meaning to our own lives – and understand ourselves – as we do the people in other stories, by connecting their background to what they choose to do, what plans they have for the future, what happens to them, and not least what relationships they have with other people. To tell the story of yourself is to become yourself.

The problem, of course, is that we are not exactly truthful narrators. We have a tendency to magnify the good things we've done while minimizing the bad. We move the negative behaviour further back in time and the good behaviour closer to the present. When I tell myself and other people about myself, I will normally try to steer clear of the bad things and stay close to the good. I also like to attribute to myself better motives than I really have. There is a system to these displacements. I will appear more frequently in a better light. Not because everything negative has been eliminated, but there's no doubt that often my recollections will have passed through some beautifying filter. Being aware of this can help to keep this airbrushing somewhat under control. Sometimes we lie so convincingly to others that we start believing our own lies. They can turn into all-encompassing life lies. As La Rochefoucauld writes: 'We are so accustomed to disguise ourselves from other people, that in the end we disguise ourselves from ourselves.'[28]

I like to think that I have a good memory, but now and then I wonder if it's so good that I even have memories of things that never happened. They rarely concern anything spectacular, just small things that I have told myself and others on different occasions, which change a little each time they are told. There is then something about the story I finally end up with that doesn't quite add up, without always being able to put my finger on it, and despite the fact that I clearly remember it being that way. Unfortunately, I won't normally have any film footage to compare it with, but if I know someone who was present, I'll of course ask them, fully aware that their memory is equally fallible.

Creating false memories is relatively easy. In experiments where the subjects were asked to describe totally fictitious events that they had never witnessed, half of them had false memories about the events.[29] We can say that they were able to remember them, despite being aware at the time that these events never took place since they were made up as part of the experiment. In our ordinary lives, where we are not within the framework of an experiment like this, we will of course be more inclined to believe that what we can remember must also have happened.

By telling a lie when fully aware that you are lying, you actually become more inclined to believe that what you are saying is true.[30] It clearly has a stronger effect than if you were to merely think of a lie without telling it to anyone. By lying, you are not only persuading others to believe something that isn't true: to a degree you are persuading yourself. This can undoubtedly be a source of self-deception.

You should be wary of lying about yourself to other people, for the simple reason that you may end up believing it yourself. It can of course be nice to go through life considering yourself a far more brilliant person than you have reason to, but reality has a sad tendency to catch up with you at some point. And if you did manage to carry out the self-deception until the very end, it would of course mean going to your grave without ever having known yourself – and that, at the end of the day, would be quite sad.

FOUR

Lies and Friendship

Most of us have a friend or acquaintance who tells tall stories about themselves, who talks about the extraordinary things they have experienced, and whom you initially believe before eventually realizing that these stories just don't add up. I don't normally place too much importance on these stories, and consider them a form of entertainment. The problem is that they accumulate over the years, and the author, who undoubtedly tells other fanciful stories to their other friends and acquaintances, will lose track of them. Normally the lies will be quite innocuous, but they can erode my respect for the person telling them. Besides, it also means that, in reality, it's not *him* or *her* I get to know but an entertaining invention that he or she has created. A friendship depends on continually elaborating and interpreting yourself and your friend, which hopefully leads to a better understanding of both. The liar undermines this process. It is therefore a kind of breach of the friendship contract.

Erving Goffmann points out that when we find out that we have been dealing with a fraudster, it is like discovering that the person did not have the right to play the role he played.[1] Furthermore, he emphasizes that the better the fraudster played the role, the more provoked we are, because it weakens the connection we initially assume exists between someone's right and ability to play a role. In short: it weakens the trust we have that someone really is who they are presenting themselves to be. This is especially upsetting when someone has played the role of your friend.

For Aristotle, friendship is a necessary component of a good life, and he writes that no one would choose to live without friendship even if they otherwise had everything a human being could want.[2] However, friendship is entirely conditional on there being mutual trust. If you don't trust other people or they don't trust you, friendship is impossible.[3] You have to trust your friends. Not in every respect, because although I have to trust that my friend is honest with me, I don't for example have to trust that he is an accomplished brain surgeon who is able to cure my headache with a small operation. Trust in that sense is always conditional, but it has to be there. To fundamentally mistrust each other would be a breach of the norms of friendship. It is therefore right, as La Rochefoucauld writes, that 'It is more shameful to mistrust our friends than to be deceived by them.'[4] Mistrust shows that you are not a real friend, and if you are not a real friend, you perhaps deserved to be deceived: 'Our own mistrust justifies other people's deceptions.'[5]

Kant highlights that the basis of friendship lies in the absolute trust two people have in revealing their thoughts, secrets and feelings to each other.[6] For a friendship to be real, you have to be open with each other.[7] Not only must you be able to open up to your friend – your friend must also open up to you. We have a need to show something to others, something that we are not comfortable showing to everyone, and to have someone else do likewise with us.[8] It is a very special relationship that you can only have with one or just a few other people.[9] Without a friend, a person is completely isolated, suggests Kant.[10] But you will still be isolated if your friend mostly lies about who he is, because you will only be connecting with an illusion, and as long as you are captivated by the illusion, you'll be unaware of your isolation.

Kant perhaps exaggerates the importance of sharing secrets. For my part, I must say I don't share that many secrets with my friends simply because I don't have that many secrets to share, although I do occasionally. The secrecy aspect presents an additional truth-related problem in the friendship. A secret is shared on the condition that it isn't passed on, but what do you do if you seemingly have to choose between revealing the secret or lying to someone else? You would obviously experience a conflict of duty, and I don't think the problem has a general and satisfactory answer. However, I do think you can normally avoid the problem by simply not replying or by replying evasively. In very special circumstances, such as when witnessing under oath in court can prevent a serious offence or similar, it seems that truth has to take precedence over friendship; but in most other situations, and not least where it concerns entirely private matters, I would probably put friendship first.

For us to be friends, you don't necessarily have to share your innermost secrets – they are mostly for you alone – but you do have to share something that you don't share with everybody. We must distance ourselves from a lot of people in order to form close bonds with a few. We form relationships by choosing to reveal different aspects of ourselves and by giving others access to us in different ways. There are some things we want to keep all to ourselves. There are many things we want to share with family and friends in a setting where we can express ourselves more or less unbound by any pretence. And there are things we want to share with a much wider audience. If you share no more with me than you do with everyone else, then we are just acquaintances, not friends, because there is nothing special connecting us. There is nothing wrong with just being 'acquaintances', and I have many acquaintances I really value, but it is a different kind of relationship, something more distant and less binding than a genuine friendship. If an acquaintance turned out to be totally different to how he had presented himself, my view of him would change, but I wouldn't feel especially betrayed. With a friend it would be different. It would then be as though we had never really known each other, even if our friendship had suggested otherwise. It would be like getting a painting by the famous art forger van Meegeren instead of a real Vermeer. To put it bluntly: rather than being a friend, it would make him an impostor who has tricked his way into my life.

There are many examples, in both the world of fiction and the real world, of people whose entire lives have been built on lies, so much so that even their friends and family never really knew them. Don Draper, in the TV series *Mad Men*, stole the identity of a deceased fellow soldier from the Korean War, and used it to build himself a new life. However, maintaining an identity that isn't yours is demanding. This lie requires constant looking after simply because it cannot be supported by reality, and has to be supplemented with new lies in order for it to be sustained. Living your life based on such an intricate web of deceit, as Don Draper does, is an almost unbearable burden. A real-world example of this would be the Frenchman Jean-Claude Romand, who started off with a small lie about having passed an exam, and then, over the following eighteen years, expanded it into an all-encompassing fraud that involved telling family and friends that he was a qualified doctor and worked as a researcher at the World Health Organization.[11] Romand pretended to go to work every day, but spent most of his time just wandering around. He would now and then say he was going on a business trip, but would just go and stay at a hotel near his local airport for a few days before returning home. To stay financially afloat, he pretended, among other things, to help relatives invest their money, but instead used them to support his own livelihood. He also had a mistress. On 9 January 1993, fearing that his lying would be exposed, Romand killed his wife with a rolling pin and shot their children in the head while they slept. He then went to visit his parents, and shot them and their dog. After that he tried unsuccessfully to kill his mistress by spraying tear gas in her face and strangling her with a cord. He concluded it all with a thoroughly half-hearted suicide attempt. He served 26 years in prison and was released in 2019.

For those who lie, and have to constantly tell new lies to conceal the previous ones, their investment in the lie can eventually become so great that the cost of exposing it can seem totally insurmountable. What remains of such a consummate liar's social identity if the veil of lies is pulled aside? They would still have their private identity, the one they haven't shared with anyone else, but their social identity would be completely destroyed. The main problem with living as a liar is not just having to live with these two identities but having to keep them distinctly separate, because they cannot really coexist.

We all have a private identity that is rarely shown to the public. This even applies to those who seem to have no reservations when sharing their thoughts on social media or elsewhere. For most of us, it would be uncomfortable to have something that is reserved for our private identities revealed and made public, but it wouldn't totally undermine our social identity, as it would in the cases of Draper or Romand. It might put a scratch in our social paintwork, but it wouldn't be impossible to make it fit with someone else's general description of who I am. A crucial part of friendship lies specifically in giving another person access to something in this private identity that isn't shared with the public. Because the inveterate liar must keep his private identity totally hidden, this liar cannot have any friends. Others might think they are his or her friend, but it is an illusion.

The stories we invent about ourselves are dynamic, and today, as a fifty-year-old, I will tell a different story about who the twenty-year-old me was than I would have done as a thirty-year-old. My twenty-year-old self looks different through the eyes of a fifty-year-old than it did through the eyes of the thirty-year-old. Basic facts, such as what I studied, who my girlfriend was and where I lived, will be the same, but the events I highlight as being the most crucial will not, and I would make different connections between them. The stories of the fifty-year-old and the thirty-year-old would be different, but none of them would be a lie. A friend would perhaps correct me, pointing out that I omitted something significant or exaggerated part of my story, but he would still recognize the story as being the story of me. A friend's job is, among other things, to correct us when our stories lose their grip on reality.

What about a friend who believes his own lies? Who, for example, has lost contact with his children, and complains about how unfair this is since he was always such an excellent father to them and put their needs before everything else? It is a story he has told himself so often that he now believes it. The problem is that you know it's not true. You know that he was certainly no child abuser, but he definitely put himself and his career first, before his family, and that he was home so rarely that the children hardly knew him. It's the same story, again and again: if something doesn't go the way he wants it to, it's always unfair or someone else's mistake – it is never the result of his own shortcomings, never his responsibility that it turned out that way. A sober view from an outsider will easily determine that he is chiefly responsible for what has gone wrong. If he genuinely believes everything he's saying then I can't really accuse him of lying to me, but he is still a liar in a way, because he is lying to himself. I would be cautious about maintaining a friendship with someone like that. Not because he would be breaking with the norms of friendship, because he would not be actually lying to me even if what he is saying is untrue, but I would consider him very unreliable because of how convincingly he lies to himself. After all, if he cannot trust himself, it would be extremely difficult for me to trust him. If I were to be a good friend, I would have to try and correct his self-understanding, little by little, and try to get him to take responsibility for the life he has led. It is a vital obligation for our friends to tell us truths about ourselves, even unpleasant ones. As La Rochefoucauld points out: 'The hardest task in a friendship is not to disclose our faults to our friend, but to make him see his own.'[12]

Let's say you're out shopping and you want to buy a large full-length mirror, and there are two you can choose between. The first mirror reflects how you really look to other people. The second mirror is more advanced. It takes a photo of you which is then fed into a photo-editing program that smoothes out your wrinkles, deducts or adds a few kilograms in all the right places and makes numerous minor changes so that what you see is the most incredibly attractive version of yourself. Which mirror would you most like to have on your wall? Would you rather look at yourself in the advanced mirror or the realistic mirror before you walked out the door to face the world? The same applies to your friends. Do you want friends who always tell you what's most pleasing to your ears or friends who tell you what they really think about you? Choosing the former, the comfortable illusion, is choosing to be disconnected from reality.

The American philosopher Robert Nozick has formulated a philosophical thought experiment with what he calls an experience machine, something you can just plug yourself into for the rest of your life, and experience anything you might want. We could then all experience having wonderful families who are never a problem, be surrounded by amazing friends, beat everyone at Wimbledon and win the Champions League final, solve all kinds of political problems and make both poverty and pollution a thing of the past, write epoch-making philosophical works and, for that matter, receive a whole stack of Nobel Prizes. All this is, of course, one giant illusion, but the actual *sense* of well-being would be very real.

So the question is: would you connect yourself to such a machine? If the only relevant thing to consider is feeling good, it would be irrational not to hook oneself up. It would all seem totally real, and you would be immensely pleased with yourself. As happy as you could be, in fact. On the other hand, to not want to connect would mean you have decided that there are more important things than just feeling good: that real relationships and achievements are worth more than illusory ones. The vast majority of people say that they would not connect to such a machine.

As we have seen, however, we have a strong tendency to create personal illusions about our lives, so that our perceptions of ourselves become increasingly detached from reality. We create our own experience machines, because they are more comfortable to live in. A friend's task might then be to tear us free from the machine's embrace and put us back in touch with reality; we should be grateful for that, but it isn't always the case. La Rochefoucauld writes: 'Few people are wise enough to prefer useful criticism to treacherous praise.'[13] We should be so wise, no matter how painful it might be to hear that we have fallen short. It is good to have honest people in your life. But how can you know that they are honest? You can never be certain, but you can *feel* certain. One reason for this feeling of certainty is that these people have shown honesty in the past: they have, for example, spoken the truth in situations where it perhaps seemed easier to lie. With honest people around you, you know they will tell you when they believe you have made a mistake or done something wrong; in short, when you have fallen short of yourself. This is why you can also trust that they are sincere when they praise you. They are your marker buoys, helping you orient yourself in life.

As a friend, one has a duty to be truthful not just because you should generally be so, but because friendship itself requires a certain type of sincerity. As a friend, it is your job to tell your friends when, in your opinion, they are making bad choices or forming bad habits. That's not to say you have to constantly impose your own preferences on your friends, because that would make you an intolerable know-it-all that hardly anyone wants to be friends with, but you would be failing as a friend if you unreservedly approve everything your friend does. You need friends because you need a critical opinion of yourself from someone who knows you and wishes you the best. For a friendship to be genuine, it must be fundamentally based on mutual goodwill. There are plenty of cynical views on friendship, from Morrissey's 'We hate it when our friends become successful' to Gore Vidal's 'Whenever a friend succeeds, a little something in me dies.' These friendships have fallen short if that's the case. When a true friend criticizes you, you know that the criticism is well-intentioned. It can hurt and you might not necessarily agree, but it is criticism you should take seriously. If you only accept praise from your friends, you have no friends.

And if you are a notorious liar, you cannot expect to make that many friends. Plato writes:

> Now of all things good, truth holds the first place among gods and men alike. For him who is to know felicity and happiness, my prayer is that he may be endowed with it from the first, that he may live all the longer a true man. For such a man is trusty, whereas he that loves voluntary deception is untrustworthy, and he that loves involuntary, a fool, and neither lot is to be envied. For sure, the traitor or the fool is a man of no friends. Course of time discovers him and he prepares for himself utter loneliness in the trials of age at the end of his days, so living equally destitute of companions and children, whether they survive or not.[14]

There is something right about Plato's emphasis on how the liar becomes solitary. One thing is that people tend to avoid people if they notice that they are lying – we prefer to surround ourselves with those we believe we can trust, and you cannot trust a liar. What's equally important is that a liar will cut themself off from other people, because they must hide their inner self from other people.

FIVE

The Politics of Lying

When discussing lies and politics, I'm not primarily concerned with investigating the extent of lying in politics, but rather the normative question of whether, and if so when, it is acceptable to lie in politics.

Speaking from the parliamentary lectern, the former Norwegian prime minister Per Borten said that sometimes a prime minister has not only a right, but a duty to lie. Lying may seem necessary in politics without there being a separate ethic for politicians with different rules than for everyone else. Political decisions can have far greater consequences than the decisions we make as individuals, and therefore even greater consideration should be given as to whether a lie can be in any way defended. Our political responsibilities may require a violation of our ordinary moral rules against lying.

We can distinguish between three main views on the place of lying in politics:

1 Lying has no legitimate place anywhere, not even in politics.
2 Although being honest is preferable, one should resort to lying if it's beneficial, either for oneself or the state.
3 Lying is wrong, but in politics it is still sometimes necessary.

Kant is the clearest representative of the first view. Machiavelli is without doubt a leading figure in the development of the second view. Plato can also be regarded as representative of such a view, although in a more limited sense, in that the decisive factor should always be what's best for the state and the common good, while the grounds for Machiavelli's considerations are far more self-serving. The third view is that of the German sociologist Max Weber.

We have dealt with Kant in detail already, and won't be repeating his arguments here. His all-out ban on lying is as valid for an active politician as it is for an ordinary citizen, and although there is perhaps more at stake in political matters, it is not relevant to his ethical analysis, where the decisive factor is the *type* of action, not its consequences.

Philosophical expositions on the role of lying in political life often refer to Plato's *Republic* as the first text in which this was a topic. In the *Republic*, Plato argues that it would be right to tell the citizens an untrue story about how the republic's social classes have come about, since it will make the citizens 'more inclined to care for the state and one another'.[1] How the Greek term *gennaion pseudos* in Plato's text should be translated is highly disputed, but the most common translations are 'noble lie', 'noble myth', 'noble fiction' or 'noble untruth'. It is quite surprising that Plato defended the use of such lies while otherwise putting such great emphasis on truth. He seems to defend the liar more than the lie itself. There are people whose wisdom makes them capable of judging when lying to those less wise than themselves is justified. He writes: 'But further we must surely prize truth most highly. For if we were right in what we were just saying and falsehood is in very deed useless to gods, but to men useful as a remedy or form of medicine, it is obvious that such a thing must be assigned to physicians, and laymen should have nothing to do with it.'[2] In the world of ideals, there is no room for lying. But in the concrete reality, where not all people are simply embodiments of the highest ideals, correctly dosed lies can function as a 'medicine' to make people behave as they should. However, only the wisest are capable of judging when and how lying should be done: 'The rulers then of the city may, if anybody, fitly lie on account of enemies or citizens for the benefit of the state; no others may have anything to do with it.'[3] Lies told by ordinary citizens must be cracked down on.[4] The republic's leaders, and only they, are granted permission to tell lies. Furthermore, it should be emphasized that Plato's defence of the political lie is not limited to leaders being able to tell one big lie about the republic's origins. They can lie about anything that seems beneficial, such as justifying why the state should exercise strict control over who should have children with whom, in order to breed children of the best possible quality. 'It seems likely that our rulers will have to make considerable use of falsehood and deception for the benefit of their subjects. We said, I believe, that the use of that sort of thing was in the category of medicine.'[5] The idea seems to be that the wise leaders of the republic know the truth, and so their souls will not be infected by the lies issuing from their mouths. Because of their wisdom they will also be able to consider when it is right to supply 'the masses', who do not know the truth, with the appropriate amount of lies as medicine. There seems to be no limit to the number of lies that leaders can tell the people, provided that their lying benefits the republic and therefore its citizens. Again, it should be emphasized that Plato is not defending the use of lies in general, and that he stresses, as mentioned, that the everyday liar has quite an unsuccessful life and is doomed to loneliness.[6]

Machiavelli has no problem whatsoever with political lies. He claims that being truthful should be commended, but that in politics one must always be prepared to lie and deceive when it is to one's advantage.[7] According to Machiavelli, humans will always prove themselves evil unless compelled by necessity to be virtuous.[8] In the long run, absolutely everyone will turn out to be evil, and therefore even a prince must use all the evil means that are useful to him. Kindness – since humans are largely evil – will lead to self-destruction. Using lies and deception against those who would use it against you is legitimate, he claims; since he has already established that people are inherently evil and cannot be trusted, there's nothing preventing such means from being used when the opportunity arises. Since you cannot assume that others will be honest with you, you do not have to be honest with them.

Thomas Hobbes is also open to the use of lying in politics. As Hobbes sees it, the state's most important tool of governance is fear. He writes that no emotion makes people less inclined to break the law than fear.[9] The state threatens its citizens with punishment, and the fear of this punishment ensures that these citizens coexist peacefully.[10] Hobbes's basic idea is that citizens should be willing to submit because they believe it will serve their interests. So the state must ensure that people fear the right things, and it must direct this fear appropriately, to convince the citizens that certain things should be feared more than others, since the people won't automatically fear what's most expedient from the state's perspective. Hobbes points out that this may require a degree of image management on the part of the state, to magnify certain phenomena and downplay others. Lying is thus a legitimate tool of governance from Hobbes's perspective. However, he claims that the state must be truthful about its own basis of government. He thus does not accept a platonic, 'noble' lie when it comes to the basis of state power and the rights and duties of citizens.[11] On this matter, those in power have a duty to tell citizens the truth. Nevertheless, those in power are free to lie to the citizens about whatever they might otherwise find useful. Nor does Hobbes accept that general freedom of speech or academic freedom can be used to speak out against those in power. Rulers should be fully permitted to regulate in detail what pupils and students should learn.[12] For Hobbes, as for

Plato, it is concern for the stability of the state that makes lying legitimate. Hobbes argues that anyone teaching a philosophy that is contrary to the law can be justifiably punished, even if the philosophy happens to be true.[13] This means that politics takes precedence over truth, and the state can lie if it serves its interests. At the same time, it must be stressed that Hobbes's formulation presupposes that there is such a thing as truth, separate from political interests. For totalitarian regimes, such independent truth does not exist.

Max Weber has a different approach, in which he tries to manoeuvre himself into an intermediate position between moral politics and realpolitik, one that falls between an idealistic demand that in politics only the most morally high-value means are permissible, and a cynical view where in principle any means is acceptable if it serves one's purpose. Weber writes:

> We have to understand that ethically oriented activity can follow two fundamentally different, irreconcilably opposed maxims. It can follow the 'ethic of principled conviction' or the 'ethic of responsibility'. It is not that the ethic of conviction is identical to irresponsibility, nor that the ethic of responsibility means the absence of principled conviction – there is of course no question of that. But there is a profound opposition between acting by the maxim of the ethic of conviction (putting it in religious terms: 'The Christian does what is right and places the outcome in God's hands'), and acting by the maxim of the ethic of responsibility, which means that one must answer for the (foreseeable) *consequences* of one's actions.[14]

Weber will say that Kantian ethics are indefensible in politics, while Machiavellian ethics are unethical. As mentioned, Kant is perhaps the leading representative of an ethical view where moral duties are given such superior validity that lying to save another person's life is forbidden. The ethical absolutist can always say that they acted according to their ethics, but that the circumstances led to an unfortunate result. The responsible ethicist highlights that here they must also take into account the consequences of their actions; they are themself contributing to a number of causes, well aware that the consequences can be serious. The ethics of conviction and the ethics of responsibility are not polar opposites but instead complement each other, and sometimes, Weber claims, the ethics of conviction must be suspended for the sake of being responsible. The problem is that there is no theory that can tell us exactly when it is right to suspend the norms of the ethics of principled conviction. Weber writes:

> No ethics in the world can get round the fact that the achievement of 'good' ends is in many cases tied to the necessity of employing morally suspect or at least morally dangerous means, and that one must reckon with the possibility or even likelihood of evil side-effects. Nor can any ethic in the world determine when and to what extent the ethically good end 'sanctifies' the ethically dangerous means and side-effects.[15]

One's judgement must inevitably be used when making this decision, since there is no ethical theory that can tell you exactly when consideration of the consequences should override the moral rules that otherwise apply. Such a Weberian view might also be called 'weak consequentialism'.[16] Where a normal consequentialist position says that you should always act in a way that has the best possible consequences, weak consequentialism says that one should normally follow the ethics of principled conviction, although there may be cases where the consequences of doing so will be so unacceptable that consequences will take precedence over principles.

Weber explicitly thematizes the demand for truth, and writes sarcastically about how the ethics of principled conviction views the case:

> Finally, there is the duty to be truthful. For the ethic of absolute principles this is an unconditional duty. Hence it was concluded that all documents should be published, especially those which placed a burden of guilt on our country, and that a confession of guilt should be made on the basis of these documents – unilaterally, unconditionally, regardless of the consequences. The politician will take the view that the upshot of this will not serve the cause of truth, but rather that truth will certainly be obscured by the misuse of the documents and by the passions they unleash. He will take the view that the only productive approach would be a systematic, comprehensive investigation, conducted by disinterested parties; any other way of proceeding could have consequences for the nation which could not be repaired in decades. 'Consequences', however, are no concern of absolutist ethics.[17]

Weber points out that politics is a dirty business, and anyone wanting to act responsibly in this particular world must be willing to get his hands dirty. The ethical paradox of getting 'dirty hands' is that you sometimes have to do something wrong to do something right. As far as truth and lies are concerned, it means that while it's wrong to lie, the political circumstances may compel you to. The question then is: when can and when should one do it? And the short answer to that is: as rarely as possible, and only when the consequences of being honest would be very bad for the nation.

A capable politician can hardly avoid getting his hands dirty. A wholehearted Kantian who always lives by the categorical imperative will in too many situations deprive himself of the means required to achieve goals that are of great political importance. If you can't imagine yourself breaking any moral rules, you probably shouldn't enter high-level politics. The price you pay for a life in politics is the certainty that there will be times when you have to act immorally because it is the right thing to do. For Weber, the 'responsible' politician is someone who acts immorally and feels burdened by it. This is quite different from having double standards, since this politician accepts morality as binding for him, but still chooses to break with it for weightier reasons. He is a slightly tragic figure. He knows that lying is wrong, he acknowledges it and feels great discomfort in doing so, but knows that he is still required to do it in order to fulfil the task he has undertaken. In special circumstances, such as while a country is in serious danger over a long period, getting dirty may be necessary more often, but it should be avoided as much as possible and reserved for only the most serious cases.

A Weberian ethics of responsibility can never defend lies told primarily for one's own benefit. But political lies are often specifically for the benefit of the politician, even though they are justified as being in the nation's interests. The politician is then either lying to avoid public opposition, to retain power, or to serve the interests of whichever party he or she sympathizes with. Secrecy justified on the grounds of national security is often intended not so much to prevent the enemy from acquiring knowledge as it is to stop its own population from getting it. When attempts were made to hide the so-called Pentagon Papers, it wasn't to prevent the Viet Cong from learning about the development of the USA's war in Vietnam, since the Viet Cong would have been fully aware of that already; it was to prevent the American people from knowing, because it could weaken public support for the war. The purpose of the secrecy was thus to suppress public knowledge of something that should without question have been the subject of democratic control. The lies told by the Nixon administration would never have met Weber's requirements for an ethics of responsibility.

All the thinkers we have so far considered write within a horizon where the political lies are specific, where someone has lied to justify a particular course of action – such as going to war – or to hide something specific that may be unfavourable to the regime. Hannah Arendt believed that she could see a new type of lying in the modern age, which she found was especially typified by Nazism and Communism. More specifically, it was a form of lying that sought not only to cover up certain truths, but to nullify the very distinction between truth and untruth: 'The lies of totalitarian movements, invented for the moment, as well as the forgeries committed by totalitarian regimes, are secondary to this fundamental attitude that excludes the very distinction between truth and falsehood.'[18] Among other things, Arendt relied on the observations of Alexandre Koyré, who in an essay in 1945 wrote that modern man, in a totalitarian society, 'bathes in the lie, breathes the lie, is in thrall to the lie every moment of his existence'.[19] He goes on to say that 'the totalitarian regime is based on the *primacy of the lie*.' We can say that the totalitarian lie is characterized by how absolutely effortless it is. Within a totalitarian mindset, there is nothing questionable about lying. Instead of double standards, it is entirely devoid of morality.

Arendt emphasizes that where the traditional lie was about secrecy, the modern lie will concern something that is clear to everyone; where a story will be rewritten before the very eyes of the person actually experiencing it.[20] It is not about covering up reality but about destroying reality, so that reality cannot confront the lie. The traditional, political lie was about winning a debate or covering up certain facts at the expense of the truth, while the modern lie is about supplanting reality itself.[21] Arendt claimed that the concentration camps were a striking example of how a totalitarian regime makes rules and constructs a reality that *becomes* truth.[22] An expression of this is a phrase from an anonymous diary found in Auschwitz: 'We're not human beings anymore, nor have we become animals; we are just some strange psycho-physical product made in Germany.'[23] The dehumanization processes in the concentration camps were intended to show that the Jews were not fully fledged human beings. For example, by making prisoners wallow in their own shit – in Bergen-Belsen, 30,000 women shared one latrine – they became ostensibly identical to the shit. The prisoners were forced into a reality where they became proof of the regime's propaganda.

Totalitarianism came up with a radical idea, based on the traditional concept of truth embodied in the correspondence between mind and reality: We can produce truth if we can produce reality! Instead of the mind attempting to grasp a reality, it should produce a reality. In other words, we don't have to 'wait until reality unveils itself and shows us its true face, but can bring into being a reality whose structures will be known to us from the beginning because the whole thing is our product'.[24] The modern liar is not first and foremost a thinker, but a *creator*, one who sets actions in motion, so that a politician's words *become* truth even if they are not yet truth.

If you can control 'reality' in that way, you can also control those living in that reality. Arendt writes:

> What makes it possible for a totalitarian or any other dictatorship to rule is that people are not informed; how can you have an opinion if you are not informed? If everybody always lies to you, the consequence is not that you believe the lies, but rather that nobody believes anything any longer. This is because lies, by their very nature, have to be changed, and a lying government has constantly to rewrite its own history. On the receiving end you get not only one lie – a lie

which you could go on for the rest of your days – but you get a great number of lies, depending on how the political wind blows. And a people that no longer can believe anything cannot make up its mind. It is deprived not only of its capacity to act but also of its capacity to think and to judge. And with such a people you can then do what you please.[25]

A society where 'everybody always lies' might seem inconceivable, but the point of Arendt's exaggeration is that the lying in such societies would be so widespread that everything would be unreliable. One would lose one's grip on reality.

Totalitarianism breaks down social space, and by doing so the distinction between what's private and public. Arendt describes it as 'organized loneliness'.[26] There are demonstrable differences between democracies and totalitarian, or authoritarian, societies in terms of trust and interpersonal relationships. It is, incidentally, a point anticipated by Aristotle, who points out that friendship exists only to a small degree within tyrannies and to a large degree within democracies.[27] In a society so permeated by lies, it becomes almost impossible for people to direct their trust anywhere. To function as citizens, they need the 'trusting and trustworthy company of my equals'.[28]

In totalitarian societies, everyone is forced to lie – the leaders must lie to the people if they want to retain power, and the people must lie about believing the lies. Whether it concerns facts or values, an opinion deviating from those expressed by the political leaders is not just *another* opinion, but a *wrong* and *dangerous* opinion threatening to undermine the entire structure of society. We can say that this society has, as a whole, been made into a giant echo chamber. Those expressing divergent opinions must therefore be punished, whether by imprisonment, committing them to a mental hospital, forced labour or death – something which in addition sends a clear message to the rest of the population that there is only one 'truth', and that it's best to comply if you don't want to be seen as a liar or an enemy of the people. If you are going to be part of the community, you must lie about believing the lies. The same phenomenon can be observed on a smaller scale with cults, although the punishment for dissenters here would normally be ostracism or expulsion.

A related phenomenon can be seen in the public sphere of liberal democracy, where many people express things contrary to what they believe in order to be more popular. Social pressure undoubtedly has its positive aspects, since it can regulate public behaviour, but it can also be a social force that produces conformist liars. To be part of a social community, people will publicly express opinions that differ from their own because they believe it will make them more socially acceptable. It is a well-known phenomenon, such as when a teenager claims to be a fan of an artist just because their friends and classmates are, when in reality they prefer a completely different type of music. When this dynamic occurs in the political world, rather than the aesthetic one, it is more serious, because it makes people highly disinclined to think differently. Democracy needs friction. One of liberal democracy's crucial obligations is to promote dialogue in the public sphere, and this dialogue doesn't work optimally when it runs too smoothly. For democracy, having too many people agreeing too much is never a good thing. Such group dynamics have a tendency to be self-reinforcing, narrowing the scope as to which beliefs and statements can be seen as legitimate. In liberal democracy, the rule of law and fundamental rights are the most important tools for guaranteeing that people have room for freedom of thought, but the rule of law can fall short when faced with social pressure. Civil society, and the various groups within it, monitor and regulate themselves. So, as a member of civil society, you have to help break the spiral of purity by introducing other perceptions, if you have them.

You have a responsibility to speak the truth, both to yourself and to others. First, to simply play along would be a prime example of self-incurred immaturity. Second, you would also be helping to compound the social pressure that makes others play along too. This form of lying may seem harmless, but it is without question detrimental to liberal democracy.

Harry Frankfurt writes that democracy is especially good at producing bullshit because of 'the widespread conviction that it is the responsibility of a citizen in a democracy to have opinions about everything, or at least everything that relates to the conduct of his country's affairs'.[29] I do not agree with Frankfurt here. At the very least, I think it's worse if a country's leaders produce bullshit than if the rest of its citizens do. Here, totalitarian and authoritarian regimes are clearly far worse bullshit producers than democracies. The advantage of democracy is that the country's leaders actually have to be responsible for the people, and their bullshit will often come back to haunt them. A dictator, on the other hand, does not have to be responsible for the people – unless a revolution is taking place – and can instead dictate what is 'true'.

The only antidote to lies is truth. The truth offers resistance to politics. As Hannah Arendt writes, it is therefore 'hated by tyrants, who rightly fear competition from a coercive force they cannot monopolize'.[30] The truth is first and foremost a weapon of the weak. But truth is rarely simple, and the truth is that it can also be a weapon for the strong, and lying a weapon for the weak. For example, a government will have immense resources to help it reveal unpleasant truths about its opponents, and a dissident may need to lie in order to keep his secrets hidden. The secrets might concern the person's private life and be irrelevant politically, but they could still discredit him and leave him politically neutralized; they might, for example, be about unusual sexual preferences or infidelity within a culture that has zero tolerance for such behaviour. From the totalitarian point of view, whether this information is true or false is essentially irrelevant, because you can invent whatever truths you want.

For the opposition, it is worth maintaining that truth exists, even though this truth might also be uncomfortable for them. One advantage of having a realistic concept of truth is that we can say that reality itself justifies certain ways of talking about reality and contradicts others. This means we can rightly maintain that certain views are true no matter what power someone with a different opinion might have, be it a dictator or a democratic majority. In other words, there is a standard for judging perceptions, and this standard does not comply with the use of force. That is why it is so important for totalitarian regimes to suppress any genuine search for truth. Without truth, only might is right.

Lies in Modern Politics

Throughout the history of politics, there has been no shortage of Machiavellian, Hobbesian and Weberian lies. Even the most honest politician will lie from time to time. This is quite obvious, for example, when it comes to u.s. presidents.[31] Some have really strived to be truthful, and the clearest example of this is perhaps Jimmy Carter, who stood for election by promising the people that he would 'never tell a lie'. It should also be mentioned that Carter wasn't a successful president, and served only one presidential term. Carter did try to keep his promise, which occasionally caused him a lot of trouble, but he didn't manage to completely avoid lying. His press secretary, Jody Powell, defended lying on a limited basis: 'From the first day the first reporter asked the first tough question of a government official, there has been a debate about whether government has the right to lie. It does. In certain circumstances, government not only has the right but a positive obligation to lie. In four years in the White House I faced such circumstances twice.'[32] In one of those circumstances, the lie was motivated by a desire to spare the pain and embarrassment of innocent people, and the other concerned the military's plan to rescue American hostages in Iran. Powell wasn't exactly a habitual liar, and nor was his boss. Carter was perhaps too much of a moralist politician and too little of a realist to be a successful president. His successors have been far more flexible with the truth. For example, there's no doubt that the Bush administration lied to justify the invasion of Iraq.[33] It claimed that there was rock-solid evidence that Saddam Hussein was a close ally of Osama bin Laden, and that it was unquestionably true that Iraq had weapons of mass destruction. This wasn't true, and the Bush administration knew it wasn't true. They may have believed that Saddam had weapons of mass destruction, or at least that he was about to have them, but they knew that there was no solid evidence for making such a claim, which means that claiming to know this for sure was a lie. And the connection between Saddam and Osama was pure fantasy.

What was special about the Bush administration's lying before the invasion of Iraq was how they targeted not only their own people, but the heads of state from other countries. As the American political scientist John J. Mearsheimer points out, heads of state and diplomats rarely lie to each other.[34] He initially thought the opposite was true, but changed his mind after studying the subject further. He admits that there are of course examples of them lying to each other, but that these are exceptions rather than the rule. It is difficult to successfully lie to other heads of state because they usually have a lot of information about the subject or will make sure they get it. Often, there will be so little trust between the countries that no claim will be believed without good documentation, which is especially true if the countries are not allies. 'Trust, but verify.' This phrase, often attributed to Ronald Reagan, is actually an old Russian proverb: *Doveryai, no proveryai.* The president started using it during his talks with Mikhail Gorbachev, after someone suggested he learn some Russian proverbs to create a good atmosphere during the negotiations. Reagan was enamoured of the proverb, and repeated it so often that Gorbachev grew tired of hearing it. Either way, trust doesn't run deep if every claim has to be verified.

If a head of state lies a lot, it will make future cooperation difficult because no one really wants to enter into an agreement with someone they cannot trust. In fact Henry Kissinger rejected the use of deception in political negotiations,[35] the reason being that you have to relate to the same people over and over again, and even if you succeed in deceiving them once, you will have destroyed the relationship and made any future negotiations very hard to conduct. However, it should be said that Kissinger had quite a flexible relationship with the truth, to put it mildly. No one would describe him as uncompromisingly honest. Stalin was at least honest when he said that, in his opinion, the truth had no function whatsoever in diplomacy, that it was in fact as impossible as 'dry water'.

Heads of state lie more often to the leaders of friendly countries or even allies, than to leaders of rival countries, if they believe it serves their interests. For example, Israel lied to both its friends – such as the United States – and enemies about its nuclear weapons programme. Israel has never officially confirmed that it has nuclear weapons, although that it does have them is probably the worst-kept secret within international security politics. When heads of state lie to each other they will, for example, do so by exaggerating their military capability to create a deterrent, or by downplaying their military capability so they can build them up without outside interference. Getting away with such a lie can hurt in the long run. The Soviet Union successfully convinced the United States that it had a far greater arsenal of cruise missiles than it actually had. The problem for the Soviet Union was that its supposed military resources were so worryingly large it made the United States significantly escalate the arms race, which in turn led the Soviet Union to use far greater resources than it had intended in order to keep up. Financially, the arms race broke the back of the Soviet Union. The lie – told to ensure the state's continued existence – wound up strongly contributing to its downfall. Another example is how Greece lied about its budget deficit in order to gain access to the Eurozone. One of the entry requirements was for Greece's budget deficit to be less than 3 per cent, but its actual deficit was vastly higher. Greece itself denied lying, but claimed that the misinformation had resulted from a mix-up in the state accounts. Either way, the fact remains that Greece provided false information about public finances, for which the country was severely punished during the 2008 financial crisis and the years that followed.

On the other hand, Mearsheimer stresses that on matters of foreign policy heads of state lie far more often to their own citizens. They may have the best motives, such as when Franklin D. Roosevelt lied to the American people in order to ensure the United States' participation in the Second World War. Roosevelt rightly feared that Germany would otherwise succeed in occupying the whole of Europe, and therefore said that the Germans had attacked the ship uss *Greer* in September 1941. He had the best intentions, and the outcome was good. But we can nevertheless still question whether the lie was acceptable. From a utilitarian perspective, it was undoubtedly so, but it can be argued that the population had a right not to be lied to, and that Roosevelt violated this right.

Mearsheimer claims that foreign policy lies are usually forgiven or even applauded by the population if the results are good – or at least not that bad – but that stronger condemnation is normally directed towards domestic policy lies. He explains this difference by saying that the head of state's most important task is to ensure the state's survival. In foreign policy, countries are in an almost Hobbesian state of nature characterized by the war of all against all, and there is no global police force a state can call upon if it gets into trouble. An individual state must therefore resort to the necessary means, including lies and deception, to ensure its own survival. The field of domestic policy, however, has a different arrangement where citizens turn to the state itself for protection, and so lying and deception cannot be justified for the same reasons as they are in foreign policy. A simple explanation for this, which Mearsheimer doesn't mention, is that in foreign policy there is a sense of 'us against them', while in domestic policy it's easier for it to be more like 'us against the state'.

An important type of political lie is the nation-builder that often evokes a heroic past where every stain – even genocide – is washed away. These lies can be considered variants of Plato's 'noble lie'. Every country has likely used a degree of 'creative' history writing, because in every country there is a desire to promote unity by strengthening national pride. Some countries go further than others. For example, in Russia it is striking how, under Putin, drastic steps have been taken to airbrush everything the Soviet Union did during the Second World War, so that it can be used in Russian nation-building. Such history writing can be especially problematic in multi-ethnic societies where there have been serious conflicts between different groups. In Bosnian schools, pupils – depending on whether they are 'Bosnian', 'Serbian' or 'Croatian' – have different curricula for 'national issues', which applies not least to how the events of Yugoslavia's civil war in the 1990s are portrayed. This would appear to be a perfect recipe for prolonging the conflicts between these groups. In many countries, nation-building lies are warmly embraced quite simply because the people want to hear them.

That the citizens of other countries don't believe these lies is of secondary importance. When a government protests now and then about how their country is being portrayed in another country, it is more to convince its own citizens than anyone abroad. If one could successfully convince the citizens of other countries, it would be a bonus, not something one can expect, for the simple reason that another country's citizens will rarely have the same incentive to believe the lies. You will always be able to reach *some* foreigners, and most countries even have a handful of enthusiasts happy to believe North Korean propaganda, but they are quite marginal. There are exceptions of course, where a glorifying portrayal of a country has been successfully sold to a broad foreign audience, such as the Chávez regime's eulogy of the 'Bolivarian Revolution' in Venezuela. Even so, it's the home crowd that matters. Such lies are of minimal risk for most politicians. The public are far less appreciative of liars who try to cover up incompetence, corruption or some other criminal act, as Richard Nixon found out during the Watergate scandal.

Power corrupts, and that applies to politicians who have good intentions as well as those who don't. How can we trust the intentions of someone who lies to us? They may have convinced themselves that they have the best intentions, but it's not inconceivable that more suspicious motives are at play. And if we were to trust their motives, how can we trust their judgement? When a government lies, the citizens lose an essential part of the chance to protest or, for that matter, give the policy their informed endorsement. Lying is fundamentally at odds with the essence of democracy. This is obvious when it comes to black lies, but it's not necessarily any less problematic with the presumably well-meaning lies that I might tell you because I think it's in your best interests. The altruistic lie is a paternalistic lie, and it can have enormous reach in the political domain, where a government can lie to the people on the grounds that it is in the people's best interests. The paternalist assumes that citizens are like children who cannot be relied on to form sensible opinions. Telling political lies to one's own population is incompatible with genuine democracy because it deprives people of the opportunity to make free choices, since these choices have to be informed. Lying to the population is more or less the same as subjecting them to coercion.

Lying is incompatible with the idea of democracy and an inevitable fact in the reality of democracy. Liberal democracy is based on criticism – on the fact that all citizens have the right to express their views on how society develops and about what is unsustainable – and it is also contingent on them having access to verifiable information. The American philosopher John Rawls's principle of public reason dictates that the authorities should not be able to pursue a policy that they are not able or willing to defend publicly to the citizens.[36] In modern democratic theory, a fundamental principle is that the considerations of political bodies should be as public as possible. If the public has no insight, it has only a minimal chance of holding the authorities responsible for a policy they are pursuing; partly because they don't always know *what* policy is being pursued, and partly because they don't know *why* it is being pursued. Secrecy is therefore at odds with democracy. At the same time, it is clear that some secrecy is unavoidable for reasons of national security, privacy and so on. Secrecy, however, is quite different to lying. Can the need for secrecy be used to justify lying too?

Can it ever be legitimate for a government or public authority to lie to its citizens? The British philosopher Glen Newey takes this point so far as to claim that under certain circumstances the citizens of democratic states have a *right* to be lied to.[37] His argument is that if a government has a duty to implement a measure – and if this measure can only be implemented if a government gives the public a false impression by lying – then a government has a duty to lie, and the citizens a right to be lied to. It is further assumed that the citizens have given prior consent to being lied to in particular circumstances, such as when national security is at stake. In isolation, it is a plausible argument. If I ask you to lie to me, I have revoked my right to not be lied to. If you also have a duty towards me, and you can only fulfil this duty by lying to me, you will have a duty to lie. Of course, the problem is that if we agreed that you should lie then I wouldn't believe you. The same would apply to a state: if the citizens have accepted that the state is lying to them because the citizens themselves have asked the state to do so, their confidence in the state being truthful will be significantly lessened, and the effect of the lie would be lost. Another problem is that the citizens have never consented to being lied to, and I find it hard to imagine, for example, a referendum being held on the state's right to lie. Second, such a policy requires the citizens to be exceptionally trusting of the state, more specifically that the government should only lie in situations which the citizens have deemed acceptable. How can citizens know that a government with the option to lie does so only when national security is at stake? If we look at many of the lies that have been exposed in modern American politics – most famously Watergate, the Iran-Contra affair, the Iraq invasion – they were more often motivated by the interests of those in power than they were by national interests. Besides, an expression like 'national interests' is so flexible, it can accommodate far too many things.

Trump – A Totalitarian Liar in a Liberal Democracy

When talking about lying and politics, it is impossible to avoid Donald Trump.[38] All u.s. presidents have lied. Ronald Reagan, for example, made a vast number of false claims, but he was nowhere near Trump's league. Trump stands out from his predecessors. Where former presidents once told strategic lies about specific issues, Trump lied about practically everything, from the most trivial details to the gravest security and health policy issues. One of the funny things about Trump's lying was that so much of it was so obvious, such as the claim about the number of people at his presidential inauguration. It shows a contempt for reality that we have otherwise only seen in totalitarian regimes. As president, Trump told totalitarian lies within the framework of a liberal democracy, and it constituted such a marked violation of the established rules of the game that both his political opponents and critics in the press were at a loss about what to do with him.

Trump is not alone in lying. Putin, for example, has a relaxed relationship with the truth, to put it mildly, and won't hesitate in flatly denying something that's obviously true, like the fact that Russia was involved in the shooting down of a Malaysia Airlines plane over Ukraine on 17 July 2014, killing 298 people. We can hardly say Putin has more respect for the truth than Trump, but he gets away with it more easily because he has essentially succeeded in eliminating Russia's critical press. Trump would also have preferred to be rid of the critical press, which he described as the main enemy of the American people, but he was unable to do so. According to the *Washington Post* – which attempted to keep track of Trump's lying during his years as president – Trump lied or made very misleading claims on 30,000 occasions. And this is merely an overview of his public communications – it doesn't include the lying he does in private or behind closed doors.

It is, of course, a question of interpretation as to how much a claim must deviate from the facts for it to be untrue or very misleading, but it would be quite uncontroversial to claim that no former u.s. president has been less truthful than Trump. Strictly speaking, we cannot say for sure that Trump was lying. We can see that he made false assertions at breathtaking speed, but to determine if he was lying, being truthy or talking bullshit, we would need to know his state of mind, and we don't. We know it only indirectly, through his words and actions.

Trump is an unsophisticated speaker – he is no master of traditional political rhetoric where one can avoid telling the truth by distorting the truth instead of lying – and this has proven to be one of his strengths as a politician. During the U.S. election campaign in 2016, I had to take a three-hour drive from Washington to a university in Virginia where I was to give a guest lecture. At this point the Republicans still hadn't chosen their candidate, but several polls indicated that Trump was doing well. Personally I'd taken it for granted that he wouldn't be the Republican candidate, and the idea that he could be the USA's next president had barely crossed my mind. Over the course of the journey, I started considering it differently. My driver, an entirely normal and friendly guy – the brother of the chief of police in the city where the university was located – was a Trump supporter. This surprised me, because at that point I had still not met anybody, or at least anybody in their right mind, who considered him a good presidential candidate. My driver was without question in his right mind. His most important reason for Trump being his favourite was because 'he tells it like it is!' What gave Trump an advantage over all the other candidates was his honesty. It wasn't hard to agree that the other candidates didn't seem all that trustworthy, on both the Republican and Democratic sides. But while I considered Trump to be someone who made the other candidates' untrustworthiness pale in comparison, my driver saw things differently. Because Trump stood out from the other candidates, my driver saw him as the real truth-teller in a sea of corruption.

Trump supporters, those who thought he did a good job as president, consistently outnumbered those who found him trustworthy. One way of interpreting this is that these citizens believe that honesty is of secondary importance – because all politicians are perceived as dishonest, for example – which means that one has to rely on other criteria. In the United States, public trust in the mass media has been plummeting for years, and this distrust is strongest among Republican voters. In such a climate, a citizen will not view the mass media as a trustworthy alternative to the Trump administration's claims, even if the same citizen also thinks the Trump administration is untrustworthy.

In the USA, the most iconic presidents have been admired for their exceptional truthfulness. It begins with the story of how George Washington as a child simply could not tell a lie about having chopped down a cherry tree. Ironically, the story itself was a lie. It was one of Washington's early biographers, Mason Locke Weems, who made it up because it suited the tribute he wanted to write. In fact, even the anecdote was a plagiarism, stolen from the Scottish writer and philosopher James Beattie's work *The Minstrel*. In any case, honesty has long been considered a virtue, but no president has been further from embodying this virtue than Donald Trump.

When Ronald Reagan finally admitted his involvement in the Iran-Contra scandal, he made the following statement: 'I told the American people I did not trade arms for hostages. My heart and my best intentions tell me that's true, but the facts and evidence tell me it is not.' This contradiction between the facts and what one *feels* is true is striking, and was a precursor for Trump, but Reagan at least acknowledged that facts do exist and that they can show something other than what one's feelings are saying. Reagan thus upheld the distinction between truth and truthiness. In the Trump regime, this contradiction melted away. It did not recognize that there is an independent reality that could contradict what the Trump administration may at any time decide to claim. Where others would normally come up with an excuse – admit that they were wrong perhaps, if what they say was proven to be untrue – Trump chose instead to simply repeat the claim, seemingly unaffected by what the facts might indicate. His preference for a certain claim simply weighed heavier on him than the facts, and he would not allow himself to be corrected by reality.

If confronted with the fact that something he had said was untrue, instead of substantiating his allegation, his strategy was to claim – usually with no further justification – that the person making the criticism was not credible, thus implying that the criticism is not credible either and should therefore be considered irrelevant. We can say that this strategy is not intended to promote one's own credibility, but instead to undermine the credibility of any critical voices. If nobody can be trusted, you may as well believe Trump just as much as you do the *Washington Post*.

Trump seems to be the incarnation of what is called 'post-truth'. Oxford Dictionaries chose 'Post-truth' as its word of the year in 2016, claiming that it relates to circumstances where objective facts are less important in shaping public opinion than appeals to personal emotions and beliefs. One interpretation of 'post-truth' is that it describes a situation where our language, judgements and claims don't refer to anything we can call facts or reality. Defining 'facts' or 'reality' isn't terribly simple either. Personally, I like how the American science fiction writer Philip K. Dick defines reality as something that doesn't go away even when you stop believing in it. The crucial thing this definition captures is that reality transcends our perceptions of it, and that it can therefore serve as a corrective to them. If our claims lack such a corrective, then our language can be no more than a strategic game. There will be no standard for the various stories to be evaluated against. If we have abandoned truth in favour of post-truth, we have also put lying behind us. If by lying we mean claiming that something is different to what one actually believes, it presupposes that one believes that something *is* actually one way or another. Post-truth, on the other hand, specifically denies that something actually *is* one way or another, that there are instead only linguistic utterances that work strategically.

We are all more inclined to absorb information from sources with the same values as ourselves and to disregard sources with other values. We do this even if – based on the usual criteria for scientific validity – there is more reason to trust the latter in a given case. We are not so open to accepting the existence of valuable information that is contrary to our own beliefs. This confirmation bias is, however, something we can try to counteract by directing ourselves towards a broader supply of information. In a world where truth still has authority – where we accept the distinction between what we *believe* is true and what *is* true – there are still correctives to our confirmation bias, but in a world of post-truth it is given unrestricted leeway.

In a study by the PEW Research Center, 76 per cent of Democratic voters in the 2016 presidential election claimed that they would be unable to agree with Republican voters on basic facts, while 81 per cent of Republican voters claimed the same.[39] As the voters saw it, this wasn't just about incompatible values or incompatible views on what would be the best political decisions, but about an unresolvable disagreement about the facts themselves. Value polarization leads to factual polarization. It illustrates how facts and values influence each other, even though there is a logical distinction between them. A person's values will have an effect on what they consider to be the relevant facts, and what they consider to be the facts will co-determine what values that person has. This produces not just group values, but also group facts. Are you going to believe CNN or Fox News?

One would initially think that disagreements over facts can be resolved by referring to what research says, but it is not always that simple. In many cases it's quite easy to settle a disagreement about factual issues. If you and I disagree on what the atomic weight of gold is or whether it can go rusty, we could easily determine what's true by consulting a quality-assured source. It becomes instantly more complicated when values are involved, because expert knowledge in this area is not accepted in the same way. Although logically there is a watertight distinction between facts and values – you cannot derive values from facts or vice versa – in practice they will have an effect on each other because one's values will influence what one perceives to be the relevant facts, and what the facts are perceived to be will co-determine the values one has.

It's possible to have rational discussions about both facts and values, and about the connection between the two. The big problems arise when values start overruling facts; when they lead to someone becoming unreceptive to facts that contradict their beliefs. In short, the problem is that it becomes far too easy for values to not just influence the facts but override them. Not principally in the sense that politicians simply 'invent' facts that are convenient for them – even if they often do, and not least in Trump's case – but more often in the sense that they are so selective in their use of facts that it cannot be described as anything other than fraudulent or quite simply a lie.

In such a polarized universe, those with different beliefs are not people you associate with to reach a presumably reasonable opinion. They are enemies. We raise our echo chambers to a societal level. Trump's much-talked-about wall that was supposed to run along the USA's border with Mexico in reality goes right through America's population. It is this 'wall' that enabled Trump to get away with the stream of provable lies as much as he did. It is unlikely that the majority of his supporters embraced post-truth despite the fact that the Trump administration did. Most people do care about what's true and what's false, and do not see language solely as a tool in a purely strategic game where you can score points. There appears to be some form of self-deception among Trump's followers, where they choose to believe in him because they *want* to believe in him and disregard anything that to an outsider would indicate that he is devoid of credibility.

As previously mentioned, we cannot determine with certainty whether Trump's untruths should be categorized as lies, bullshit or truthiness, but we can at least establish that his handling of the truth is not an example of Weberian ethics of responsibility – it is instead Machiavellian realpolitik. Furthermore, it is also a completely different format to anything we have ever seen in a liberal democracy.

SIX

Living with Lying

We don't need to have a reason for telling the truth, but we do need a reason for lying.[1] We would simply rather tell the truth if we can achieve what we want by doing so. The need for lying arises when we have to deal with a problem that the truth would have caused us.

This asymmetry concerns not only the speaker but the listener too. You need a reason to assume that someone is lying. As a rule, you will assume that people are telling the truth. Since people mostly do tell the truth, you'd be doing the right thing. And as a rule, you will continue to do so, but you might also find reasons to doubt or dismiss something. For example, you might be concerned that I have a history of being a notorious liar; that I have a great deal to gain from you believing me, and that it would be a great inconvenience to me if things were not how I said they were. It might just seem implausible because it contradicts many of your own perceptions. Either way, you need *reasons* to believe that I am lying.

In *The Ethical Demand* (1956) the Danish philosopher and theologian K. E. Løgstrup writes:

> It is a characteristic of human life that we normally encounter one another with natural trust. This is true not only in the case of persons who are well acquainted with one another but also in the case of complete strangers. Only because of some special circumstance

do we ever distrust a stranger in advance ... Initially we believe one another's word; initially we trust one another. It may indeed seem strange, but it is a part of what it means to be human. Human life could hardly exist if it were otherwise. We would simply not be able to live, our lives would be impaired and wither away if we were in advance to distrust one another, if we were to suspect the other of thievery and falsehood from the very outset.[2]

As Løgstrup sees it, such trust is a fundamental requirement of being human. We don't initially *decide* to trust someone – we just do. Trust comes first, it is a given, and you need a reason to replace it with mistrust.

When we more rationally consider whether we should give others our trust, we see that there are many circumstances where trusting that a person isn't lying is totally unproblematic; not least when it's in the mutual interests of both parties to be honest with each other, for example collaborating on something where both are dependent on the other successfully completing their tasks. We also have good reason to trust strangers who have nothing to gain from being dishonest. There can, however, also be situations where we have good reason to be more doubtful. As the German philosopher and sociologist Georg Simmel points out, trust is rarely absolute – we will normally have a *degree* of trust in someone.[3] The fact that I trust you're not lying doesn't necessarily mean I have to trust that you're being truthful. For a highly specialized question – like assessing epidemiological data during a global pandemic – should you lack this expertise I wouldn't have to rely on your speculations, even if you were being totally sincere.

A huge amount of our knowledge is based on trust. Everyone has to rely on information from other citizens, journalists, experts and so on. All of these people must in turn trust others, and experts must trust other experts' assessments of each other. Since we cannot personally guarantee that those who are supposed to be upholding the truth really are doing so – because ultimately it would require us to be as knowledgeable as they are, and in that case we wouldn't need them – we have to trust other authorities who tell us which authorities we can trust. In that sense, a great many of the things we think we know are based on acts of faith, where we have chosen to believe some things, but not others. We cannot, each and every one of us, personally determine what's true, from the ground up. We inevitably have to rely on authorities. The question is: which authorities?

What separates reflective trust from naive trust is the fact that I am also open to counter-perceptions: I am open to the possibility that you perhaps don't know what you are talking about or that you are lying. In order to make that assumption, however, I need to have a reason, and such reasons are seldom present during the trivial interactions of our daily lives. Without such reasons, it is normally appropriate to just assume that someone is telling the truth. It lowers the transaction costs when dealing with each other, sparing us from having all sorts of assurances complicating the way we interact. People who trust each other can socialize with an immediacy that is non-existent in a climate of mistrust. Simmel claims that society would simply disintegrate without peoples' general trust for each other.[4] He therefore describes trust as 'one of the most important synthetic forces within society'.[5] A society devoid of mutual trust would not be a proper society but a collection of isolated individuals who have to be constantly wary of each other. Truthfulness is a prerequisite for civilization. Without respect for the truth, we no longer have reason to trust each other, and without that, civilization will deteriorate. If we cannot trust that we are conveying reliable information to each other, we cannot rely on it. There is always a risk when interacting with others. Trust is based on an act of faith that enables you to deal with this uncertainty and actually interact. When trust is eroded, it leaves only isolated groups and individuals.

We need a basic level of trust if we are to communicate with each other at all. If we can't assume that other people are mostly telling the truth, communication will break down. The assumption of truth is a necessary requirement for understanding. I have to assume that most of the claims you make are true, otherwise the reality you are describing would have no connection with my reality. If we were living in two different realities, we wouldn't be able to understand each other. It's impossible to imagine someone who only ever lies and yet is capable of sustaining a communicative relationship. Lying, by definition, has to be a sub-phenomenon, a deviation. We have to assume that most communication is truthful.

If you imagine a normal day, where you talk to family, friends and colleagues, receive emails, read newspapers, watch television, talk to shop assistants and so on, you are clearly the recipient of a huge amount of claims stating that something is like this or like that. Unless it is a special case – especially if someone claims something that conflicts with what you otherwise believe is true – you will take it for granted that people are honest. Our general attitude towards each other is that we are not looking to deceive each other by lying. It would be hard to do otherwise. Try imagining what a normal day would be like if you instead assumed that people are mostly dishonest. You would find it near impossible to do anything that involves other people.

The short answer to the question of who can you trust is: most people, most of the time. As mentioned, most people lie less often than average.[6] Social psychological studies indicate that on average people lie in about 25 per cent of their interactions on a normal day. These averages, however, are misleading because while a majority of the participants in the studies lie very rarely, a minority lie very often, which means that the latter group raises the average. The notorious liars pushing this figure higher are not representative. So a minority are responsible for most of the lying, while the majority account for very little of it. In that sense, it is typical for us humans to be quite truthful. Studies on the frequency of lying are also constructed to produce high numbers. The studies estimating lies at every fourth interaction are designed such that a conversation must last at least ten minutes without the occurrence of a lie in order for it to be categorized as 'honest', while any conversation, no matter how brief it is, will be categorized as 'dishonest' if it contains even one lie. In the bigger picture, of all the things we say to each other, lies make up a very small proportion.

It is for this precise reason that a liar can succeed in his endeavour. It allows the lying minority to sponge off the trust created by the honest majority. Lies cannot succeed without trust. So it would be prudent even for a liar to be honest most of the time and dish out the lies sparingly, because no one will trust someone who has proven to be a notorious liar. As Hannah Arendt points out, a liar has one great advantage over an honest person: he knows beforehand what his audience is expecting to hear, and can adapt his message accordingly instead of having to conform to a reality that might sometimes appear far less plausible than the lie.[7]

Lying is a violation of the trust we need in order to work together. As Montaigne puts it:

> Our understanding is conducted solely by means of the word: anyone who falsifies it betrays public society. It is the only tool by which we communicate our wishes and our thoughts; it is our soul's interpreter: if we lack that, we can no longer hold together; we can no longer know each other. When words deceive us, it breaks all intercourse and loosens the bonds of our polity.[8]

Since lying is such a serious phenomenon, it would be nice if there was a simple formula for exposing liars. But there isn't one. There are no techniques you can learn that will help expose a liar while they are lying to you. Most lies are exposed afterwards. If you study the literature about the different signs that might indicate someone is lying, you will find that they don't really exist. There is a widespread cross-cultural belief that people who are lying avoid eye contact, but there is no scientific evidence of this.[9] Sometimes liars will look you straight in the eye, sometimes they won't. Someone telling the truth might look you in the eye, or they might not. It is a worthless criterion for distinguishing between liars and truth-tellers. The same applies to behavioural traits such as unfriendliness, uncertainty and hesitation.[10] Such behaviour causes people to trust a speaker less, but this is completely unrelated to whether they are actually honest or dishonest. If you appear friendly, composed, confident and committed, people are more likely to think you are honest, but even that has no connection to whether you actually *are* honest. We can predict, with some precision, which speakers will be perceived as honest or dishonest, but that does not help us decide which speakers are actually telling the truth and which ones are not. If there is any proof that some signs can indicate lying, it would be that liars' voices more often rise in pitch and their pupils dilate a little, but not even this gives us better lie-detecting powers. People who are trained to expose liars get slightly better at identifying them, but at the same time they become slightly worse at identifying people who are telling the truth, which makes them no more accurate in general.[11] It is tempting to say that their training hasn't made them experts at distinguishing between honest and dishonest people, but has simply made them more suspicious.

In studies where people were asked to consider if someone was lying or telling the truth, the level of accuracy was only slightly better – around 54 per cent – than if they had tossed a coin. Statistically, this is not insignificant, but it is too low to be of any notable practical use. The reason for us being slightly, but not much, more effective than what pure coincidence suggests could be because while some liars are quite incompetent and will openly reveal themselves, most liars are quite clever.

It should also be pointed out that in these situations the test subjects know that there is a fairly high probability that they are being lied to. In our daily lives, we rarely have that attitude towards others. We instead act on the unreflective assumption that people mostly tell the truth, and since we are poor lie detectors this means that reasonably competent liars will get away with their lying most of the time. Incidentally, spontaneous lies succeed marginally better than premeditated ones.

There is hardly any connection between *seeming* honest and *being* honest. Most people who seem honest are honest, but most of those who are dishonest also seem honest. Some people who seem dishonest are actually honest, and of course there are hopeless liars who both seem and are dishonest. You can observe the same behaviour in a liar as you would in someone who is honest, and observe behaviour you would associate with honesty in a liar. 'Signs' of honesty and dishonesty are really quite worthless. The most you can learn from studying these signs is how to become a better liar, not how to get better at detecting one. You can learn how to appear more honest, but it won't help you decide who actually *is* honest.

If you want to become a better lie detector, there is only one thing to do: pay less attention to how people *behave* when they say something, and focus more on *what* they are actually saying. First, does what they are saying sound plausible based on what you otherwise believe? Do they have evidence for what they are claiming? Second, it might help of course to know a little about whether this person is normally honest or not. It is *facts*, first and foremost, that expose the liar, not the liar's behaviour, except for those cases where the liar admits his offence voluntarily of course. Either way, if you are going to expose a liar, it is not the liar's inner life but the actual facts that you should focus on. Both the speaker *and* the listener have a responsibility to evaluate whether what's being said is true.

As mentioned, it is generally wise to assume that people are telling the truth, simply because they mostly do. You will be fooled occasionally, but it is better to be fooled occasionally than to go through life without trusting anyone. A trustless life is a lonely one. How we think about truth and lies affects what kind of self-understanding we have, our relationships with others, and the society we live in. In the Book of Psalms (116:11) it says: 'All men are liars.' But although this may be true, it is more accurate to say that most people are fairly honest. Just not all the time.

We may condemn lying, but that doesn't mean that we should go to the opposite extreme and insist upon always telling each other the whole and full truth. If we all told each other everything we were thinking, we would find each other unbearable. We have to conceal things from other people, and we have to make a distinction between what's private and what's public. As Georg Simmel highlights, social relationships require a certain amount of cover-up and secrecy – the amount of which will vary depending on the type of relationship – and he regards lying as a primitive expression of this necessity.[12] Kant is on the same page in his *Anthropology*. He writes that we could imagine the beings on an alien planet who are only able to think out loud; in other words, they have to express everything they are thinking.[13] Unless they were pure angels, he writes, they would be unable to tolerate each other – they would be unable to form a community. A human community requires a certain degree of pretence. As we have seen, Kant believes that concealing one's thoughts is acceptable, but lying is not.

Truth is not so important for much of our daily communication, and often just functions as interpersonal 'glue'. Our language can be used for so many other things, which in many contexts can be significantly more important than telling the truth. A person who insists on us finding the profound and absolute truth about every case, and at every opportunity – for example, at a party while chatting informally over a glass of wine – breaking away from the social norms of associating with others, will eventually become quite intolerable and also find that the number of party invitations they get dwindle considerably. Not only are there pathological liars, there are pathological truth-tellers who lack any understanding of social relations, which would suggest that you don't *always* have to tell the whole truth, or that it might be at least considerate to resort to a euphemism or something similar now and then. If you have been asked to give an after-dinner speech, people will expect you to express yourself differently to how you might do so in a restaurant review. Critical remarks about how the sauce was too salty and the meat too dry have no place in such a speech. Obituaries will usually present the most favourable description of whoever has passed away. To describe the deceased as a talentless, unreliable asshole would normally be regarded as a grave violation of what's customary, even if it is actually true. There are many contexts where lies and bullshit are both accepted and expected, and where they do very little harm. Telling the truth is not a speaker's primary task in some contexts, and this is something that both the speaker and the audience usually fully understand.

As mentioned, it is only lying when the listener has reasonable grounds to expect the speaker to be truthful. To lie might seem like a easy solution to a problem, but it often isn't in the long run. Lying requires a level of upkeep that truthfulness has no need for. You have to watch what you say and monitor yourself to make sure you don't reveal yourself. If you have lied to several people, and especially if the lies don't completely match, it puts huge demands on how you deal with a situation where several of these people are there at once. As a liar, it is harder to be totally present mentally when meeting other people, because your self-monitoring will undermine the immediacy that is so characteristic of having a genuine connection. Lying doesn't just potentially harm the relationships other people have with you, in that your lies might get revealed. It also damages your relationships with *them*, because lies create distance. If you have been telling the truth, you don't have to think about these things.

Kafka points out: 'One tells as few lies as possible only by telling as few lies as possible, and not by having the least possible opportunity to do so.'[14] His point is that truthfulness has to be rooted in yourself, and not in external circumstances. If you only acted rightly because the external circumstances prevented you from acting wrongly, you haven't developed any character. An important reason for not lying, even about the most trivial matters, is that you otherwise become a *liar*. You become used to lying. Aristotle highlights that moral learning mainly involves learning to feel what's right, in the right manner, at the right time. By lying repeatedly, you will unlearn yourself how to feel right. Recent neuroscience also supports Aristotle on this point. Repeatedly lying reduces the number of brain signals that make us feel uncomfortable when we lie.[15] In short, it becomes easier for you to lie without feeling guilty or uncomfortable.

Not only that, but we suffer from the delusion that by knowing ourselves we will also know others. In reality, we're such notorious self-deceivers that we hardly know ourselves at all. Yet we assume that we can apply what we understand of ourselves to other people. We know, for example, that one's self-image with regards to violence is decisive for whether one resorts to violence or not.[16] Those who consider themselves violent largely interpret other people as violent and far more commonly believe that violence is therefore legitimate in given situations. Similarly, we find that people who deceive others also perceive others to be more deceitful than honest people do.[17] He who lies, and therefore cannot be trusted, also believes that others lie and therefore cannot be trusted either. And because other people cannot be trusted, the conclusion is that lying to them is legitimate. The lying becomes self-reinforcing. A liar lives in a different world to an honest person, you could say, in an untrustworthy world instead of a trustworthy one. The truth is that other people can be trusted in general, but by lying, the liar also undermines his own faith in it being so, and with every lie the liar tells, he will experience living in an increasingly less trustworthy world. It is not a good life.

I cannot think of one instance of me benefiting from someone lying to me. My knowledge is of course limited to the times I became aware of the lie afterwards, and it's quite possible there have been cases where a lie has done me the world of good, but I seriously doubt it. Nor can I think of any cases where, in the long run, someone has benefited from my lying to them. That doesn't mean that every lie I've told has caused irreparable damage – most have been totally harmless – although I wish I had chosen other solutions on those occasions.

Perhaps truthiness is a bigger problem than lying. More so than premeditated deception, it is our mental laziness – the fact that we don't bother checking to see if what we believe to be true really *is* true – that is the main source of falsehood when we interact with each other. Yet lying is more outrageous because it is such a major breach of trust. When I lie to you, I turn to you and ask for your goodwill, to be believed, and I then use that against you.

We have a moral duty to strive to be truthful, both to others and to ourselves. What's most important is not the truth, because the truth is beyond our control. It is only because truth doesn't conform to our will and desires that it exists at all. On the other hand, truthfulness is something we can to a far greater extent turn into the object of our will. You do not need an advanced theory about truth to fulfil the two virtues of truth: sincerity and accuracy. It is enough for you to say how you believe something to be, and that you make a reasonable effort to check that it really is that way. It is something that all of us should be able to do, but in practice we all fall short from time to time.

References

Introduction

1 Timothy R. Levine, *Duped: Truth-Default Theory and the Social Science of Lying and Deception*, Tuscaloosa: The University of Alabama Press 2020, ch. 9.

2 For a good overview of the research, see Jörg Meibauer, ed., *The Oxford Handbook of Lying*, Oxford: Oxford University Press 2018.

3 For a short overview, see Bella M. Depaulo, 'Lying in Social Psychology', in Jörg Meibauer, ed., *The Oxford Handbook of Lying*, Oxford: Oxford University Press 2018.

ONE What Is Lying?

1 Arne Næss, *'Truth' as Conceived by Those Who Are Not Professional Philosophers*, texts published by Det Norske Videnskaps-Akademi i Oslo Il. Hist.-Filos. Klass 1938 No. 4, Oslo: Jacob Dybwad 1938.

2 Aristotle, *Metaphysics*, trans. W. D. Ross, in *The Complete Works of Aristotle II*, Princeton, Princeton University Press 1985, 1011b25.

3 Bernard Williams, *Truth and Truthfulness: An Essay in Genealogy*, Princeton: Princeton University Press 2002.

4 Immanuel Kant, 'An Answer to the Question: "What is Enlightenment?"', in *Kant: Political Writings*, trans. H. B. Nisbet, Cambridge: Cambridge University Press 1991, p. 54.

5 Augustine, 'Enchiridion' and 'De Mendacio', in Kevin DeLapp and Jeremy Henkel, ed., *Lying and Truthfulness*, Indianapolis/Cambridge: Hackett Publishing Company 2016, pp. 4–35.

6 Immanuel Kant, *Critique of the Power of Judgement*, trans. Paul Guyer and Eric Matthews, Cambridge: Cambridge University Press 2002, §53.

7 Ludwig Wittgenstein, *Philosophical Investigations*, trans. G.E.M. Anscombe, Oxford: Blackwell: 1963, §249.

8 Ibid., §580.

9 George Orwell, 'Politics and the English Language', *Horizon*, 76/1946.

10 George Orwell, *Nineteen Eighty-Four: A Novel*, London: Secker & Warburg 1949.

11 Harry Frankfurt, 'On Bullshit', in *The Importance of What We Care About*, Cambridge: Cambridge University Press 1988, p. 130.

TWO The Ethics of Lying

1 Sissela Bok, *Lying: Moral Choice in Public and Private Life*, New York: Vintage Books 1979.

2 Aristotle, *Nicomachean Ethics*, trans. W. D. Ross, *The Complete Works of Aristotle II*, Princeton, Princeton University Press 1985, 1011b25, 1127a30.

3 Ibid., 1127a27.

4 Ibid., 1127b4–8.

5 Aristotle, *Rhetoric*, trans. W. Rhys Roberts, in *The Complete Works of Aristotle II*, Princeton, Princeton University Press 1985, 1417b36–1418a1.

6 Hugo Grotius, *The Law of War and Peace*, trans. Francis W. Kelsey, in Kevin DeLapp and Jeremy Henkel, ed., *Lying and Truthfulness*, Indianapolis/Cambridge: Hackett Publishing Company 2016, pp. 38–52.

7 Blaise Pascal, *The Provincial Letters*, trans. A. J. Krailsheimer, London: Penguin Books 1988, 9th letter, p. 140f.

8 Augustine, *Enchiridion* and *De mendacio*, pp. 4–35.

9 Thomas Aquinas, *Summa theologiae*, in Kevin DeLapp and Jeremy Henkel, ed., *Lying and Truthfulness*, Indianapolis/Cambridge: Hackett Publishing Company 2016, pp. 158–84.

10 Immanuel Kant, *Groundwork of the Metaphysics of Morals*, trans. Mary Gregor, Cambridge: Cambridge University Press 2011, p. 402.

11 Immanuel Kant, *Anthropology From a Pragmatic Point of View*, trans. Mary J. Gregor, The Hague: Martinus Nijhoff 1974, §14. Immanuel Kant, *The Metaphysics of Morals*, trans. Mary Gregor, Cambridge: Cambridge University Press 1991, p. 431.

12 Immanuel Kant, *Lectures on Ethics*, trans. Peter Heath, Cambridge: Cambridge University Press 1997, p. 700.

13 Kant, *Lectures on Ethics*, p. 62.

14 Kant, *Anthropology From a Pragmatic Point of View*, p. 332.

15 Kant, *Lectures on Ethics*, p. 446ff.

16 Kant, *The Metaphysics of Morals*, p. 429. Kant, *Lectures on Ethics*, pp. 604f., 700.

17 Kant, *The Metaphysics of Morals*, p. 429.

18 Ibid., p. 426.

19 Immanuel Kant, 'Über ein vermeintes Recht aus Menschenliebe zu lügen', in *Kants gesammelte Schriften*, vol. viii, Preußischen Akademie der Wissenschaften, ed. de Gruyter, Berlin/New York 1902–, p. 426.

20 Kant, *Groundwork of the Metaphysics of Morals*, p. 421.

21 Ibid., p. 429.

22 Baruch Spinoza, *The Ethics and Selected Letters*, trans. Seymour Feldman, Indianapolis: Hackett 1982, E4p72, p. 195.

23 Kant, 'Über ein vermeintes Recht aus Menschenliebe zu lügen'.

24 Ibid., p. 427.

25 Ibid., pp. 426, 429.

26 Williams, *Truth and Truthfulness*, p. 110.

27 Ibid., p. 115.

28 Arthur Schopenhauer, *Die Welt als Wille und Vorstellung I*, *Sämtliche Werke, Band I*, Frankfurt a.M., Suhrkamp Verlag 1986, pp. 461–6; Arthur Schopenhauer, *Über die Grundlage der Moral, Sämtliche Werke, Band III*, Frankfurt a.M., Suhrkamp Verlag, 1986, pp. 755–9.

29 Jeremy Bentham, *An Introduction to the Principles of Morals and Legislation*, London: Methuen, 1982 (1789).

30 John Stuart Mill, 'Bentham', in *Essays on Ethics, Religion and Society*, London: Routledge 1969, p. 112.

31 John Stuart Mill, *Utilitarianism*, in *Essays on Ethics, Religion and Society*, London: Routledge 1969, p. 223.

32 John Stuart Mill, 'Whewell on Moral Philosophy', in *Essays on Ethics, Religion and Society*, London: Routledge 1969, p. 182.

33 Bok, *Lying*, p. 115.

34 Michel de Montaigne, 'On Liars', in *The Complete Essays*, trans. M. A. Screech, London: Penguin Books 1991, p. 35.

35 Adam Smith, *The Theory of Moral Sentiments*, Glasgow Edition, vol. I, Indianapolis: Liberty Fund 1976, p. 338.

THREE Lying to Yourself

1 Robert Trivers, *The Folly of Fools: The Logic of Deceit and Self-Deception in Human Life*, New York: Basic Books 2011.

2 Friedrich Nietzsche, *Human, All Too Human*, trans. R. J. Hollingdale, Cambridge: Cambridge University Press 1996, §52, p. 40.

3 K. Patricia Cross, 'Not Can But Will College Teachers Be Improved?', *New Directions for Higher Education*, 17/1977.

4 Emily Pronin, Daniel Y. Lin, and Lee Ross, 'The Bias Blind Spot: Perceptions of Bias in Self Versus Others', *Personality and Social Psychology Bulletin*, 3/2002.

5 Bernard Williams, 'Truth, Politics, and Self-Deception', *Social Research*, 3/1996, p. 606.

6 Blaise Pascal, *Pensées and Other Writings*, trans. Honor Levi, Oxford: Oxford University Press 1999, p. 179.

7 Jean-Jacques Rousseau, *The Reveries of the Solitary Walker*, trans. Charles E. Butterworth, Indianapolis: Hackett Publishing Company, Indianapolis 1992, p. 44.

8 On the friendship and feud between Rousseau and Hume, see David Edmonds and John Eidinow, *Rousseau's Dog: A Tale of Two Great Thinkers at War in the Age of Enlightenment*, London: Faber & Faber 2007.

9 Rousseau, *The Reveries of the Solitary Walker*, p. 84.

10 Jean-Jacques Rousseau, *The Confessions and Correspondence, Including the Letters to Malherbes*, general ed. Christopher Kelly, Hanover/London: University Press of New England 1995, p. 551f.

11 Rousseau, *The Confessions and Correspondence*, pp. 289, 300.

12 Ibid., p. 433.

13 Rousseau, *The Reveries of the Solitary Walker*, p. 53.

14 In his *Confessions*, he claims that he spoke freely about this to everybody. (Rousseau, *The Confessions and Correspondence*, p. 300.)

15 Rousseau, *The Reveries of the Solitary Walker*, p. 52.
16 Ibid., p. 57.
17 Quoted from Joanna Bourke, *An Intimate History of Killing: Face-to-Face Killing in Twentieth-Century Warfare*, London: Granta Books 1999, p. 171f.
18 Rousseau, *The Reveries of the Solitary Walker*, p. 1.
19 Smith, *The Theory of Moral Sentiments*, p. 84.
20 Ibid., p. 110.
21 Ibid., p. 153.
22 Ibid., p. 113f.
23 Ibid., p. 158f.
24 T. S. Eliot, *The Complete Poems and Plays*, London/Boston: Faber & Faber 1969, p. 14.
25 Erving Goffman, *The Presentation of Self in Everyday Life*, New York: Doubleday 1959.
26 Kant, *Anthropology From a Pragmatic Point of View*, §14, p. 151.
27 Cf. Paul Ricoeur, *Oneself as Another*, trans. Kathleen Blamey, Chicago: University of Chicago Press 1992.
28 François de La Rochefoucauld, *Collected Maxims and other Reflections*, trans. E. H. and A. M. Blackmore and Francine Giguére, Oxford: Oxford University Press 2007, §119.
29 Quin M. Chrobak and Maria S. Zaragoza, 'Inventing Stories: Forcing Witnesses to Fabricate Entire Fictitious Events Leads to Freely Reported False Memories', *Psychonomic Bulletin and Review*, 15/2008.
30 Danielle Polage, 'The Effect of Telling Lies on Belief in the Truth', *Europe's Journal of Psychology*, 4/2017.

FOUR Lies and Friendship

1 Erving Goffman, *The Presentation of Self in Everyday Life*, New York: Doubleday 1959, p. 59.
2 Aristotle, *Nicomachean Ethics*, 1099a31–b7, 1155a22–6, 1169b10.
3 Aristotle, *Eudemian Ethics*, trans. J. Solomon, *The Complete Works of Aristotle II*, Princeton, Princeton University Press 1985, 1237b11–30.
4 La Rochefoucauld, *Collected Maxims*, §84.
5 Ibid., §86.
6 Kant, *The Metaphysics of Morals*, p. 471. Kant, *Lectures on Ethics*, p. 425f.

7 Kant, *Lectures on Ethics*, p. 679.

8 Kant, *The Metaphysics of Morals*, p. 471f.

9 Kant, ibid., p. 471.

10 Kant, *Lectures on Ethics*, p. 430.

11 Emmanuel Carrère, *The Adversary,* trans. Linda Coverdale, London: Picador 2002.

12 La Rochefoucauld, *Collected Maxims*, §410.

13 Ibid., §147.

14 Plato, *Laws*, trans. A. E. Taylor, *Plato: Collected Dialogues*, Princeton: Princeton University Press 1989, 730c.

FIVE The Politics of Lying

1 Plato, *Republic*, trans. Paul Shorey, *Plato: Collected Dialogues*, Princeton: Princeton University Press 1989, 415d.

2 Ibid., 389b.

3 Ibid., 389b–c.

4 Ibid., 389d.

5 Ibid., 459c–d.

6 Plato, *Laws*, 730c.

7 Niccolò Machiavelli, *The Prince*, trans. Peter Bondanella, Oxford: Oxford University Press 2005, ch. XVIII. Cf. Niccolò Machiavelli, *Discourses On Livy*, trans. Harvey C. Mansfield and Nathan Tarcov, Chicago: The University of Chicago Press 1996, Book III.xl-xlii.

8 Machiavelli, *Discourses On Livy*, Book I.iii.

9 Thomas Hobbes, *Leviathan*, Cambridge: Cambridge University Press 1991, ch. 27, p. 206.

10 Ibid., ch. 13, p. 90.

11 Ibid., ch. 30, p. 231f.

12 Ibid., ch. 42.

13 Ibid., ch. 46, p. 474.

14 Max Weber, 'The Profession and Vocation of Politics', in *Political Writings*, trans. Ronald Speirs, Cambridge: Cambridge University Press, p. 359f.

15 Ibid., p. 360.

16 On 'weak consequentialism', see Brian Barry, *Liberty and Justice*, Oxford: Clarendon Press, 1991.

17 Weber, 'The Profession and Vocation of Politics', p. 359.

18 Hannah Arendt, *Essays in Understanding*, New York: Schocken Books 1994, p. 354.

19 Alexandre Koyré, 'The Political Foundation of the Modern Lie', *Contemporary Jewish Record*, VIII/1945, s. 291.

20 Hannah Arendt, 'Truth and Politics', in *Between Past and Future: Eight Exercises in Political Thought*, New York: Viking Press 1969.

21 Hannah Arendt, *The Origins of Totalitarianism*, San Diego/New York/London: Harcourt Brace & Company 1979 (1951), p. 9.

22 Hannah Arendt, *Essays in Understanding*, New York: Schocken Books 1994, p. 147.

23 Quoted from James M. Glass, *'Life Unworthy of Life': Racial Phobia and Mass Murder in Hitler's Germany*, Basic Books, New York 1997, p. 27.

24 Arendt, *Essays in Understanding*, p. 354. Cf. Arendt, *The Origins of Totalitarianism*, pp. 385, 392.

25 Hannah Arendt, 'From an Interview', *New York Review of Books*, 26 October 1978.

26 Arendt, *The Origins of Totalitarianism*, p. 478.

27 Aristotle, *Nicomachean Ethics*, 1161b9f.

28 Arendt, *The Origins of Totalitarianism*, p. 477.

29 Harry Frankfurt, 'On Bullshit', in *The Importance of What We Care About,* Cambridge: Cambridge University Press 1988, p. 133.

30 Hannah Arendt, *'Between Past and Future. Eight Exercises in Political Thought'*, p. 241.

31 Cf. Eric Alterman, *When Presidents Lie: A History*, New York: Viking 2004.

32 Jody Powell, *The Other Side of the Story*, New York: William Morrow & Co 1984, p. 223.

33 Cf. John J. Mearsheimer, *Why Leaders Lie: The Truth About Lying in International Politics*, Oxford/New York: Oxford University Press 2013, pp. 50–55.

34 Ibid.

35 Henry Kissinger, *Years of Upheaval*, Boston: Little, Brown and Company 1982, pp. 214, 485.

36 John Rawls, *A Theory of Justice*, Cambridge, MA: Harvard University Press, 1971, p. 133; John Rawls, *Political Liberalism*, New York: Columbia University Press (1993), p. 66ff.

37 Glen Newey, 'Political Lying: A Defense', *Public Affairs Quarterly*, 2/1997.

38 The most extensive overview of Trump's public falsehoods can be found in the *Washington Post* Fact Checker Staff, *Donald Trump and His Assault on Truth: The President's Falsehoods, Misleading Claims and Flat-Out Lies*, New York: Scribner 2020.

39 Pew Research Center, 'Republicans and Democrats Agree: They Can't Agree on Basic Facts', 23 August 2018, www.pewresearch.org.

SIX Living with Lying

1 Cf. Sissela Bok, L*ying: Moral Choice in Public and Private Life*, New York: Vintage Books 1979.

2 Knud Ejler Løgstrup, *The Ethical Demand*, trans. Theodor I. Jensen, Notre Dame: University of Notre Dame Press 1997, p. 8.

3 Georg Simmel, *Philosophie des Geldes, Gesamtausgabe Band 6*, Suhrkamp, Frankfurt a.M. 1989, p. 215.

4 Ibid.

5 Georg Simmel, *Soziologie. Untersuchungen über die Formen der Vergesellschaftung, Gesamtausgabe Band 11*, Suhrkamp, Frankfurt a.M. 1989, p. 393.

6 Levine, *Duped*, ch. 9.

7 Hannah Arendt, *Crises of the Republic*, San Diego/New York/London: Harcourt Brace 1972, p. 6.

8 Michel de Montaigne, 'On Giving the Lie', in *The Complete Essays*, trans. M. A. Screech, London: Penguin Books 1991, p. 757.

9 Levine, *Duped*, p. 9.

10 Ibid., p. 248.

11 Ibid., p. 46.

12 Simmel, *Soziologie. Untersuchungen über die Formen der Vergesellschaftung*, pp. 383–414. Georg Simmel, 'Zur Psychologie und Soziologie der Lüge', in *Aufsätze und Abhandlungen 1894-1901, Gesamtausgabe Band 5*, Suhrkamp, Frankfurt a.M. 1995, pp. 406–19.

13 Kant, *Anthropology From a Pragmatic Point of View*, p. 322.

14 Franz Kafka, *Die Zürauer Aphorismen*, Frankfurt a.M. Suhrkamp 2006, §58.

15 Neil Garrett, Stephanie C. Lazzaro, Dan Ariely and Tali
     Sharot, 'The Brain Adapts to Dishonesty', *Nature Neuroscience*
     19/2016.
16 Lonnie Athens, *Violent Criminal Acts and Actors Revisited*,
     Urbana/Chicago: University of Illinois Press 1997, ch. 6 and 7.
17 Brad J. Sagarin, Kelton L. Rhoads and Robert B. Cialdini,
     'Deceiver's Distrust: Denigration as a Consequence of
     Undiscovered Deception', *Personality and Social Psychology
     Bulletin*, 11/1998.

Acknowledgements

I am in debt to to Siri Sørlie, Espen Gamlund, Erik Thorstensen, Erling Kagge and Joakim Botten for their comments on the manuscript. I take full responsibility for any inaccuracies or untruths that might be found in this book. I have tried to be truthful, but cannot rule out that some truthiness and bullshit may have crept in. However, I do hope the book is free of lies.

Index